Bible Teaching for Wisdom: *The Effective Four*

Copyright© 2021 by Danny R. Bowen and David M. Cook

Published by TeachersOfTheBible, Georgetown, KY

All rights reserved. No part of this book may be reproduced, stored in a retrieval system, or transmitted in any form or by any means — electronic, mechanical, photocopy, recording, or otherwise — without written permission of the publisher, except for brief quotations in printed reviews.

All Scripture quotations, unless otherwise indicated, are from the Christian Standard Bible®, Copyright 2017 by Holman Bible Publishers. Used by permission. Christian Standard Bible® and CSB® are federally registered trademarks of Holman Bible Publishers.

ISBN: 978-1-948667-05-0

10 9 8 7 6 5 4 3 2

Contents

Foreword	iv
Acknowledgements	vi
About the Authors	vii
Why?: The Importance of Bible Teaching	**1**
Chapter 1 — The Big Question for the Teacher	2
Chapter 2 — The Aim of the Teacher	14
Chapter 3 — Teaching for Repentance	20
Additional resources for The Importance of Bible Teaching	27
Summary: The Effective Four Questions	**28**
What?: Searching the Bible	**31**
Chapter 4 — What is the Bible?	32
Chapter 5 — How to Study the Bible	38
Chapter 6 — Resources for Studying the Bible	46
Additional Resources for Searching the Bible	54
So What?: Making It Matter	**57**
Chapter 7 — Knowing Your Learners, Part 1	58
Chapter 8 — Knowing Your Learners, Part 2	66
Chapter 9 — Transforming Your Learners	72
Additional resources for Making It Matter	82
So What Now?: Turning It into a Lesson	**85**
Chapter 10 — Helping Learners Answer the Effective Four	86
Chapter 11 — Teaching Methods	90
Chapter 12 — Measuring Change in Your Learners	98
Chapter 13 — Planning for Change in Your Teaching	104
Additional resources for Turning It into a Lesson	108

Expanding to Bigger Projects — 111
Chapter 14 — Planning a Multi-Lesson Course — 112
Chapter 15 — Planning a Multi-Course Curriculum — 116

Resources & Helps — 123
Observation Worksheet — 124
Structure worksheet — 125
Context Worksheet — 126
Interpretation Worksheet — 127
Lesson Plan Template — 128
Teaching Feedback Form — 129
Course Development — 130

Foreword

Why another book on teaching? Because, despite all the valuable resources available to teachers, much teaching in the church remains lifeless. Many of those considered the "best of the best" still teach Bible facts rather than Bible truth. Even many of those who teach straight from the biblical text fail to show their learners how the Bible applies to daily life. At the other extreme, some who do teach application jump right to personal application without regard for the truth of the passage written, as it were, to an audience far removed from us in time, language, geography, and culture.

God has given me a heart that longs for good teaching in the church. My passion is for the front-line teachers because of their impact on the bride of Christ. I have seen the problem of bad teaching but, for years, I had no solution to offer. In fact, because of some who modeled teaching for me, I was part of the problem. I was guilty of modeling bad teaching by practicing bad teaching despite the accolades I accepted for it. Then, James 3:1 convicted me. Under that conviction, I returned to school as an old guy. Through the studies for a Master of Divinity in Christian Education and a Ph.D., I have questions and answers — better questions than before and some, not all, of the answers.

> James 3:1 Not many should become teachers, my brothers, because you know that we will receive a stricter judgment.

Through God's work in my life during that season, I developed the method outlined in this book. Then I started using it to teach teachers in the church and in the academy, first at The Southern Baptist Theological Seminary and now at The Southwestern Baptist Theological Seminary. This book is an attempt to share my experience, my questions, and my answers with you. My prayer is that this effort will help you to become a better teacher of God's Word — a transformer of people rather than a dispenser of information.

If you find this book useful, you can thank God that He can use someone like me to equip you. If you find it useless, you can blame me. Better, you can let me know how it might be improved. You can reach me through TeachersOfTheBible.org.

In addition to updating several sections for clarity, in this updated book, I have added a fifth section — Expanding to Bigger Projects. In this section, there are chapters on how to use the Effective Four to turn raw content into an effective lesson as well as how to think about an overall curriculum scheme for a church.

In this revised edition of the book, my friend and one of my former students, Dr. David M. Cook, has contributed Chapters 2 and 3. In those, he took the original one chapter summary of content from my doctoral dissertation and made it more accessible.

Acknowledgements

I am indebted to the faculty of The Southern Baptist Theological Seminary for my training. Much of what you will read in this book is a product of courses from and interactions with that faculty. It is likely that many of their thoughts are echoed here without proper citation because what they have taught me has become a part of me and my teaching.

Likewise, I am indebted to the many students I have taught across a number of institutions of higher learning and teachers I have taught in a number of churches. Their questions and confusion about what I attempted to teach them have refined my thoughts presented here. Some of their teaching demonstrations have been passed on in Chapter 10.

As I mentioned in the Foreword, I am thankful for David M. Cook, a former student of mine. Dr. Dave is, I hope, the first of many students to join me in presenting, refining, and spreading this teaching method.

I am also grateful for the following teachers who reviewed the original manuscript to sharpen the book before it went to print:

Dr. Shane Parker
Laura Beville
Bryan Wilburn
Chris Day
Dr. Randy Fryar

Soli Deo Gloria

About the Authors

Danny R. Bowen, Ph.D. is a professor of educational ministries at the Southwestern Baptist Theological Seminary. With a B.S. in Nursing and a M.S. in Nurse Anesthesia, he continues as a bi-vocational healthcare provider and has contributed chapters to anesthesia textbooks and to *Practical Family Ministry: A Collection of Ideas for Your Church*. He returned to school as an old guy to earn both an M.Div. in Christian Education and a Ph.D. from The Southern Baptist Theological Seminary. He has taught for years in a variety of higher education settings and has taught for decades in the local church. His passion is to help teachers grow in their teaching ministries and, based on his doctoral dissertation, he has developed this biblically-sound, simple method of teaching the Bible. Dr. Danny is married to Penny and they have two grown children and three grandsons.

David M. Cook, D.Ed.Min. serves as Senior Pastor of Calvary Baptist Church in Greenwood, Indiana. He received an M.A. in Christian Worship, as well as a D.Ed.Min. in Leadership, from The Southern Baptist Theological Seminary. Dr. Cook is the author of "The King's Fear of the Lord as a Theme in the Books of Samuel," in *Themelios* (December 2020) and articles for 9Marks, Indianapolis Theological seminary, and Baptist Press. Dr. Dave lives in Greenwood, Indiana, with his wife Emily and their four children, where he is currently reigning house tickle-fight champion.

Why?
The Importance of Bible Teaching

Bible teaching is important because the One who commissioned it has been given authority over all heaven and earth. But why is teaching the Bible so important to Jesus? Why would he call you, me, and so many others to do it?

This first section helps you think through why you are a teacher and what you should hope to accomplish as a teacher. Getting the right perspective from the beginning will be important to teaching more successfully in the classroom as you see your learners transformed by the very lessons you prepare.

But, before God uses you to change others, let Him change you. You might be tempted to gloss over the study in Chapter 1. Please don't! Take time to answer each question posed before moving on. The heart changes in the learners I advocate for in Chapter 2 begin with the heart change in you, the teacher.

This pattern — teacher, then student — is not a new idea; it is modeled by the scribe, Ezra. When the Israelites returned from their captivity in Babylon, God appointed Ezra the teacher over the nation.

> Ezra 7:10 Now Ezra had determined in his heart to study the Law of the Lord, obey it, and teach its statutes and ordinances in Israel.

In Ezra 7:10, do you see why Ezra's ministry was blessed by God? Ezra decided to know God's Word, to live God's Word, and then to teach God's Word. My prayer as you begin this book is that you would adopt Ezra's pattern as your own, that you would set your affections on God's Word, to model its truths in your life, and then to pass on those truths to those God has entrusted to you.

This section, then, focuses on the change that comes about in your life as you consider why God has called you to the great task of teaching the Bible.

1

THE BIG QUESTION FOR THE TEACHER

If you have not asked it, there is one question that will change your teaching for the better. It can change your role from transmitter of information to transformer of hearts as the Holy Spirit works in the lives of your learners. It can change your focus from teaching the lesson to teaching the learner. This question, applicable for any field of study, is indispensable for a study of the Bible.

Once we ask and answer this question, it will form the motivation for the rest of the book. In this chapter, I'll try to help you understand the question, practice asking the question, and look for the fruit of enticing your learners to answer the question.

First, let me ask why are you — or why would you want to become — a teacher of the Bible? Don't take a lot of time to think about it, just jot down your immediate response: Why a teacher?

_____

_____

Some teach out of habit — they continue to teach because they have taught. Others teach out of convenience — they feel they need to do something and, seeing the quarterly with the lesson all prepared, they have an easy way to serve. Still others teach out of obligation — they have been guilted into the role because no one else would not say "no;" that is, they were the only ones who would say "yes." There are many more answers, good and bad. How does your answer compare? Let's do a short Bible study to help you think about your answer.

THE GREAT COMMISSION

Read Matthew 28:16–20 before continuing.

Why? — The Importance of Bible Teaching

> Matthew 28:16 The eleven disciples traveled to Galilee, to the mountain where Jesus had directed them. 17When they saw him, they worshiped, but some doubted. 18Jesus came near and said to them, "All authority has been given to me in heaven and on earth. 19Go, therefore, and make disciples of all nations, baptizing them in the name of the Father and of the Son and of the Holy Spirit, 20teaching them to observe everything I have commanded you. And remember, I am with you always, to the end of the age."

This passage is called the Great Commission. It is Jesus' final instruction to His apostles — the eleven disciples who had been with Him the longest and whose relationship to Him was closest.

The Command

Read the passage three or four times and then write down what you see as the primary command from Jesus (Spoiler alert: It is not "go"! Instead think about what we go to do).

Primary command: _____ (v. 19)

In verse 19, what is the scope of the command? That is, how far does the command extend?

Extent: _____

Now, look at the aspects of the command in verses 19 and 20. Fill in the blanks with the verbs used to describe the three aspects:

_____ (v. 19) — the heart set on obedience

_____ (v.19) — the result of receiving Christ

_____ (v. 20) — the rest of life

The main point is less clear in the English that it is in the original: the primary command is to make disciples. In verses 19 and 20, *make* is the only authoritative command. So, the Great Commission is to make disciples. That commission extends to *all nations*. We understand from other places in the Bible that the Great Commission will be effective at finding new disciples of Jesus in every nation, tongue, and tribe on the earth (Daniel 7:14; Revelation 5:9; Revelation 7:9). This is not to say that every person will be saved; only that persons from every group will follow Christ Jesus.

The actions — go(ing), baptizing, and teaching — modify the primary verb "make." So, the way we make disciples is going, baptizing, and teaching.

Going

The heart set on obedience to Jesus will go and make disciples or, more properly, will make disciples while going. This includes what is often thought of as "going on missions," short- or long-term, but it is more. It is really a life set on making disciples of Jesus wherever you go. That means that the Great Commission begins where you are and continues wherever you will be.

Baptizing

As you live out the Great Commission, you should see new disciples baptized. Being baptized is the first act of obedience for a new disciple, professing to the world what a new believer has already confessed to God.

Teaching

A disciple's profession of faith continues in obedience to Christ's commands. Because God chose to use human instruments, disciples wind up teaching other disciples, who will baptize and teach still other disciples. This pattern has continued for 2,000 years and has now been handed to you and me.

The Authority

Just one problem: we don't have what it takes. Even those who had been with Jesus during His earthly ministry were inadequate. Look at how Matthew describes at least some of them in verses 16 and 17. Some believed … yet some doubted. Despite all their personal instruction by Jesus, how could some still have doubts? The answer is simple: They are still fallen humans, imperfect in knowledge and inadequate in themselves for carrying out their responsibilities.

Why? — The Importance of Bible Teaching

If *they* were inadequate, how much more inadequate are *we* who have not spent three years walking in Jesus' physical presence?

We have neither the will nor the ability to live perfectly as disciples of Jesus or to make more disciples of Jesus. But Jesus anticipated our deficiencies. We see this in the first and last words of the Great Commission. Jot down how you see verse 18 and the last part of verse 20 connecting to verse 19.

_____

Jesus has been given all authority. The Greek word translated *all* may seem a bit tricky to some. The word translated all literally means ***all***! Jesus has all authority. That means that He has authority to delegate His work to His disciples — exactly what He does in this passage. We carry out the Great Commission under the authority of Jesus, the One who has all authority.

Jesus' Presence

Even though we have Jesus' authority, we are still inadequate to carry out our delegated responsibility. Jesus has addressed that issue in verse 20 where He promises to be with us until He returns at "the end of the age," so that we have His power to carry out the Great Commission. The command Jesus gives is sandwiched between the declaration of His authority and the promise of His presence.

> **THE GREAT COMMISSION**
> JESUS' AUTHORITY (16–18)
> JESUS' COMMAND (19–20A)
> JESUS' PRESENCE (20B)

You might have noticed the paradox — Jesus will be with us until He returns to be with us. Mark and Luke report Jesus' ascension back into heaven after giving this commission to His followers. How, then, can Jesus fulfill His promise to be with us?

> Acts 1:8 "…you will receive power when the Holy Spirit has come on you, and you will be my witnesses in Jerusalem, in all Judea and Samaria, and to the end of the earth."

Jesus answers this question in the ascension passage in Luke's second book. Look at Acts 1:8, where Jesus promises to send the Holy

Spirit, who will indwell every believer so that God the Son's presence is with us through God the Holy Spirit's indwelling.

The result of that indwelling is the next thing to notice in Acts 1:8. Jesus says, "you will be my witnesses…." Here, He is not issuing a second command. Instead, He is stating a fact. Those who are disciples of Jesus are witnesses of Jesus. The choice we have is not whether or not to be witnesses, but what kind of witnesses we will be. If you are His, you are His witness so that when family, friends, and acquaintances know you are a follower of Jesus, you are witnessing to them whether you intend to or not. That is why we need a heart set on making disciples as we go; we are either helping or hurting those we know in their knowledge of and obedience to Jesus. No wonder He put the command between declaration of His authority and the promise of His presence.

But that is not the only way Jesus is present with us. The Holy Spirit, who indwells every believer, has formed us into the church.

In 1 Corinthians 12:12–31, the Apostle Paul uses a word picture to describe our unity in diversity. He says that we are individual parts of one body, the church. In verse 27, he makes it clear, "Now you are the body of Christ, and individual members of it." Christ's body is one of the word pictures the New Testament uses for the church's relationship to Jesus. Paul restates this claim in Ephesians 1:22–23 where he says that Christ is "head over everything for the church, which is his body, the fullness of the one who fills all things in every way." He uses the same picture elsewhere (for example, see Colossians 1:18). The point, for our purposes, is that Christ is present with us as the body of believers known as the church, represented by individual churches. And, that church has been commissioned to continue to make disciples of Jesus.

The Church

Continuing our look at Acts 1:8, how does the geographical extension — "Jerusalem, in all Judea and Samaria, and to the end of the earth" — connect to the scope — "all nations" — of the Great Commission from Matthew 28:19?

Jesus is describing the order in which the gospel will spread starting from where those first disciples were. As the Roman persecution of the Jews — and

Christians, as a "sect" of the Jews — occurred, climaxing in the fall of the temple in A.D. 70, the book of Acts describes the spread of the gospel to the end of earth. The gospel was first preached in Jerusalem, where they were. Then, it extended to Judea and all Samaria, where they were going when scattered as the Romans destroyed Jerusalem and the temple located there. Finally, Acts records the extension of the gospel to "the end of the earth," where some believers, like Paul, Barnabas, you, and I would go.

As the good news was preached, on what did the new believers rely? Did they depend on experts far away or ecclesiastical leaders in the church? Take a look at Acts 2:42–47.

> Acts 2:42 They devoted themselves to the apostles' teaching, to the fellowship, to the breaking of bread, and to prayer. ⁴³Everyone was filled with awe, and many wonders and signs were being performed through the apostles. ⁴⁴Now all the believers were together and held all things in common. ⁴⁵They sold their possessions and property and distributed the proceeds to all, as any had need. ⁴⁶Every day they devoted themselves to meeting together in the temple, and broke bread from house to house. They ate their food with joyful and sincere hearts, ⁴⁷praising God and enjoying the favor of all the people. Every day the Lord added to their number those who were being saved.

In that passage, identify the first thing to which the early church devoted herself.

_____

The first believers devoted themselves to the teaching of those who had lived with Jesus for the three plus years of His earthly ministry — the apostles. How does that priority connect to the Great Commission?

_____

While being baptized is a one-time event, teaching is the ongoing work for disciples. From the time we respond to God's offer of salvation in Jesus Christ, disciples are to learn and teach others to obey Christ's commands. These commands we know because the apostles, Jesus' closest disciples, shared what they had learned from Him.

The bad news for us is that the apostles are gone. So, how can we be devoted to their teachings? The Christian New Testament, the last 27 books of the Bible, are the record of the apostles' teachings. Though the apostles are dead, their words are alive. These books were included in the Bible, in part, to document the fulfillment of promises made in the first 39 books of the Bible — the Old Testament.

With the promises made and fulfilled, we have the written Word of God complete. Without regard to any supposed "lost books," additional books claiming to "correct errors" in the Bible, or imaginations (rational or irrational), we have the complete record of God's written Word to us. No wonder those early believers held the teachings in such high regard. We cannot teach Jesus' commands without holding high the apostles' teachings — recognized by the apostles and the early church as the very Word of God — along with the Old Testament scriptures — recognized by Jesus, the Jews, the apostles, and the early church as the very Word of God.

Later in Acts, Paul became an apostle. His dramatic conversion is recorded in Acts 9, retold in Acts 22 and Acts 26, and then referenced by Paul in 1 Corinthians 9:1, 1 Corinthians 15:3–8, and Galatians 1:11–16.

Paul and the other apostles were the primary teachers in the early church. Their teaching has been passed down through every generation of believers. Take a look at 2 Timothy 3:10–17.

> 2 Timothy 3:10 But you have followed my teaching, conduct, purpose, faith, patience, love, and endurance, 11 along with the persecutions and sufferings that came to me in Antioch, Iconium, and Lystra. What persecutions I endured — and yet the Lord rescued me from them all. 12 In fact, all who want to live a godly life in Christ Jesus will be persecuted. 13 Evil people and impostors will become worse, deceiving and being deceived. 14 But as for you, continue in what you have learned and firmly believed. You know those who taught you, 15 and you know that from infancy you have known the sacred Scriptures, which are able to give you wisdom for salvation through faith in Christ Jesus. 16 All Scripture is inspired by God, and is profitable for teaching, for rebuking, for correcting, for training in righteousness, 17 so that the man of God may be complete, equipped for every good work.

Why? — The Importance of Bible Teaching

How does the Bible describe proper teaching reaching Timothy?

___

Timothy had the Old Testament as he was growing up. His mother and grandmother had taught him well (2 Timothy 1:5). Now, Timothy had Paul and other New Testament writers to draw from. Earlier in the same letter, Paul told Timothy what he was supposed to do with knowledge passed on from Paul. Read 2 Timothy 2:1–2. How does the lineage described by Paul relate to the Great Commission?

> 2 Timothy 2:1 You, therefore, my son, be strong in the grace that is in Christ Jesus. ²What you have heard from me in the presence of many witnesses, commit to faithful men who will be able to teach others also.

___

Paul, an apostle, passed on what he had learned from Jesus. Paul passed that on to Timothy, who was to pass it on to others, who would teach still others. In the span of two verses we see four generations of believers. This is the Great Commission in action. The teaching work of the apostles succeeded to a new generation of Christ-followers. That apostolic succession — succession of the teaching rather than succession of the authority of the apostles — has continued all the way down to the present time and now we are to teach what we have been taught so that other disciples can obey everything Christ has commanded.

But we are not to teach alone; God has placed us in the church. Teaching is the prerequisite to obedience and God has a plan for the church.

The Teacher

Read Ephesians 4:11–16 on the next page and answer the question that follows.

> Ephesians 4:11 And he himself gave some to be apostles, some prophets, some evangelists, some pastors and teachers, 12 equipping the saints for the work of ministry, to build up the body of Christ, 13 until we all reach unity in the faith and in the knowledge of God's Son, growing into maturity with a stature measured by Christ's fullness. 14 Then we will no longer be little children, tossed by the waves and blown around by every wind of teaching, by human cunning with cleverness in the techniques of deceit. 15 But speaking the truth in love, let us grow in every way into him who is the head — Christ. 16 From him the whole body, fitted and knit together by every supporting ligament, promotes the growth of the body for building up itself in love by the proper working of each individual part.

Who gave what to whom and for what purpose?

_____ gave _____ to the _____

so that she _____.

Christ gave, among other things, teachers to the church so that she would be equipped for ministry and be unified in the faith. If you are a teacher, Christ has given you as a gift to His bride to make her beautiful. The haunting question is "Does your teaching give what He wants her to receive?"

As teachers, we can have great confidence in our calling and the Holy Spirit's use of us as He has gifted us. How does (or how might) that confidence embolden your teaching?

_____

It is good to be confident, but confidence must be tempered to avoid pride and heresy. Read James 3:1–2 to see where some wrongly believe teachers are held to a higher standard than others in the church.

> James 3:1 Not many should become teachers, my brothers, because you know that we will receive a stricter judgment. 2 For we all stumble in many ways. If anyone does not stumble in what he says, he is mature, able also to control the whole body.

Then read 1 Peter 1:14–16 to see the standard to which all Christians are held.

> 1 Peter 1:14 As obedient children, do not be conformed to the desires of your former ignorance. 15 But as the one who called you is holy, you also are to be holy in all your conduct; 16 for it is written, Be holy, because I am holy.

What is the standard by which we are measured?

___

Our standard is God's perfect holiness. There is nothing higher so teachers cannot be held to a standard higher than perfection. Instead, teachers are held to that standard more strictly. Let's see why. Read Romans 3:9–20.

> Romans 3:9 What then? Are we any better off? Not at all! For we have already charged that both Jews and Gentiles, are all under sin, 10 as it is written: There is no one righteous, not even one. 11 There is no one who understands; there is no one who seeks God. 12 All have turned away; all alike have become worthless. There is no one who does what is good, not even one. 13 Their throat is an open grave; they deceive with their tongues. Vipers' venom is under their lips. 14 Their mouth is full of cursing and bitterness. 15 Their feet are swift to shed blood; 16 ruin and wretchedness are in their paths, 17 and the path of peace they have not known. 18 There is no fear of God before their eyes., 19 Now we know that whatever the law says, it speaks to those who are subject to the law, so that every mouth may be shut and the whole world may become subject to God's judgment. 20 For no one will be justified in his sight by the works of the law, because the knowledge of sin comes through the law.

From the passage in Romans 3, what is the problem with being measured by God's standard of perfect holiness?

___

The paradox — that we are called to holiness yet cannot achieve holiness — should humble the teacher. James is thought by some to include application commentary on Jesus' Sermon on the Mount. From the Sermon, read Matthew 5:17–20 and see for whose obedience teachers are responsible.

> Matthew 5:17 Don't think that I came to abolish the Law or the Prophets. I did not come to abolish but to fulfill. 18 For truly I tell you, until heaven and earth pass away, not the smallest letter or one stroke of a letter will pass away from the law until all things are accomplished. 19 Therefore, whoever breaks one of the least of these commands and teaches others to do the same will be called least in the kingdom of heaven. But whoever does and teaches these commands will be called great in the kingdom of heaven. 20 For I tell you, unless your righteousness surpasses that of the scribes and Pharisees, you will never get into the kingdom of heaven.

For whose obedience is the teacher responsible?

_____ and _____

As a teacher, you are responsible for your own obedience. Scarier, you are responsible in some way for the obedience of those you teach. That heavy responsibility ought to humble anyone. In fact, John, Jesus' "beloved disciple," requires humility in the teacher in 1 John 2:27.

> 1 John 2:27 As for you, the anointing you received from him remains in you, and you don't need anyone to teach you. Instead, his anointing teaches you about all things and is true and is not a lie; just as it has taught you, remain in him.

From 1 John 2:27, try to summarize in one word the necessity of human teachers:

_____

"Unnecessary" is one word that describes the necessity of human teachers. Ultimately, the Holy Spirit is the teacher of every believer so that we can know how to obey Christ's commands. However, in God's economy, He has chosen to use human teachers as His instruments of instruction. He has called teachers and gifted them to the church. That should bring great confidence in our teaching role. He has also warned teachers that the privilege is tempered with great responsibility so that we will give an accounting of our stewardship of the role. That weight ought to bring great humility and our absolute dependence on God to teach us so that we might be used to teach others.

Having completed this study and considering the balance of confidence and humility and your role in the Great Commission, answer again the original question: Why do you teach?

_____

_____

Knowing why we teach, we turn next to the heart. How does teaching change the heart so that learners obey Jesus' commands rather than simply learn things? In the next two chapters, Dr. Dave will explain why the heart, rather than the head, should be the primary target of transformation.

2

THE AIM OF THE TEACHER

It's easy to assume the primary purpose of teaching is that learners would either gain knowledge or learn a skill. This leads to sermons and Bible lessons in which Christians are taught much more about what to think and do than they are taught about what (or who) to love and desire.

This may be because teachers want measurable results, and a student's loves and desires are almost impossible to measure. We can see when our students become smarter or live differently. But how would we see a change of heart? We can't … except by seeing how they live and talk. This makes it tempting to simply feed our students facts and tell them what to do, almost like a schoolteacher is tempted to teach to the test.

Educators have words for these differences. What we might call the head, heart, and hands, they call the *cognitive*, *affective*, and *behavioral* learning domains. Knowledge is cognitive; desires and decisions are affective; and skills are behavioral. There are also big words for what happens when we get these three domains right. Cognitive learning in the head produces right belief, *orthodoxy*. Affective learning in the heart produces right desires, *orthopathy*. And behavioral learning in the hands produces right practice, *orthopraxy*.

We realize that's a lot of big words at once, so there is chart below to help keep them straight.

WISDOM			
LEARNING DOMAIN	***LEARNING AIM***	***POPULAR TERM***	***RIGHTLY ALIGNED***
Cognitive	Knowing/Thinking	Head	Orthodoxy
Affective	Desiring/Deciding	Heart	Orthopathy
Behavioral	Doing	Hands	Orthopraxy

Although knowledge and skills (cognitive and behavioral) are important, biblical wisdom includes and begins with the most often neglected learning domain: the affective domain. Wisdom begins with what we love, our desires and feelings, as well as the choices and commitments that come out of those loves.

What if, instead of producing more knowledgeable JEOPARDY!® contestants or more skilled cogs in a machine, we aim at teaching people how to be wise? What if we teach students to fear and love God, to believe the truth, and to live in obedience to Jesus?

> **WHAT IF WE AIM AT TEACHING PEOPLE HOW TO BE WISE?**

WISDOM BEGINS IN THE HEART

When teachers neglect the heart (the affective domain), we don't just miss one of three equal pillars. We miss the central foundation, the source of the other two. We can't afford to miss the heart because it is where wisdom begins.

To see this, we look at the Bible's foundational teachings on wisdom. The foundation of wisdom is laid at least five times with words similar to Proverbs 9:10, "The fear of the Lord is the beginning of wisdom, and the knowledge of the Holy One is understanding."

> Proverbs 9:10 The fear of the LORD is the beginning of wisdom, and the knowledge of the Holy One is understanding."

The author placed this verse at the center of a key stanza to emphasize its foundational role in all of wisdom. The foundation of all wisdom, "The fear of the Lord" is an affect properly disposed toward God. So, while many teaching models begin with facts or skills to be taught, the Bible begins with a heart that fears the Lord.

> "Fear of the LORD" — the beginning of wisdom — is an affect properly disposed toward God

But what is fear of the Lord? While the wisdom books help us see its foundational role, we have to zoom out and look at the whole Bible to see a full picture what it is. The many times it is mentioned add up to one simple picture: a heart that marvels at the Lord and then obeys him. We see a glimpse of God's greatness and our hearts explode with awe-filled worship. That marveling heart then begins to obey the Lord.

If wisdom begins with the fear of the Lord and the fear of the Lord begins in the heart, then it follows that Bible teaching must start with the heart. We can't teach our students to believe God's truth and walk in God's ways without teaching them to love God in their hearts.

How Hearts Change

Yet, even as we teach life-giving words, we cannot change our students' hearts. The prophets tell us who can. For example, Ezekiel reports God's promise, "I will give you a new heart and put a new spirit within you; I will remove your heart of stone and give you a heart of flesh. I will place my Spirit within you and cause you to follow my statutes and carefully observe my ordinances" (Ezekiel 36:26–27).

> Ezekiel 36:26–27 I will give you a new heart and put a new spirit within you; I will remove your heart of stone and give you a heart of flesh. I will place my Spirit within you and cause you to follow my statutes and carefully observe my ordinances.

> Jeremiah 32:40 I will make a permanent covenant with them: I will never turn away from doing good to them, and I will put fear of me in their hearts so they will never again turn away from me.

Jeremiah records a similar promise, "I will make a permanent covenant with them: I will never turn away from doing good to them, and I will put fear of me in their hearts so they will never again turn away from me" (Jeremiah 32:40).

Who do Jeremiah and Ezekiel say puts new God-fearing hearts within us?

_____

New hearts that love and obey God don't just happen — God actively gives them to us. He makes us new, what theologians call regeneration.

2 Corinthians 5:17–19 gives us a look into when and how God does that: "Therefore, if anyone is in Christ, he is a new creation; the old has passed away, and see, the new has come! Everything is from God, who has reconciled us to himself through Christ and has given us the ministry of reconciliation. That is, in

Christ, God was reconciling the world to himself, not counting their trespasses against them, and he has committed the message of reconciliation to us."

> 2 Corinthians 5:17–19 Therefore, if anyone is in Christ, he is a new creation; the old has passed away, and see, the new has come! Everything is from God, who has reconciled us to himself through Christ and has given us the ministry of reconciliation. That is, in Christ, God was reconciling the world to himself, not counting their trespasses against them, and he has committed the message of reconciliation to us.

According to verse 17, which people are made new, given new hearts?

_____

What does verse 18 say that God did through Jesus?

_____

What does verse 19 say being reconciled means?

_____

God made us new as he reconciled us to himself through Jesus. Rather than count our trespasses against us, he counted Jesus' sacrifice on the cross as a substitute. Now Jesus calls men and women everywhere to turn from sin and call upon him to be reconciled to God. This is the gospel — the good news. Those who believe upon it have been given new hearts.

The Aim

Teaching centered on the heart should be rich with this gospel because God uses it to give new hearts to stubborn sinners like you and me.

So, the aim of a Bible teacher is to see students grow in wisdom. Wisdom begins in a heart that fears the Lord, spreading into the beliefs and lives of students. Some of our students are like saplings looking to shoot up. Others are like mature oak trees that still grow a few inches each year. Still others have not been made new through the gospel. All of them need to marvel often at the Lord and his gospel in ways that engage their head, their hearts, and their hands. Fortunately, God has already placed within them a natural desire to become wise. As we will see in the next chapter, we can engage their attention by activating their God-given desire for wisdom.

3

TEACHING FOR REPENTANCE

If you had walked into the highest religious circles in first-century Israel, you would have seen haughty spirits, fake cheerfulness, divided hearts, conflict, and a quickness to jump on anyone who didn't do things just right. And, because of what these scribes and Pharisees said about themselves, you might have thought to yourself "these people are so righteous."

After a lifetime of watching them, one day you walk over to investigate an unusual crowd. They're gathered to hear a new teacher preaching on a mountainside. This teacher is not part of the rabbinic system you're used to, but He teaches with an authority you find irresistibly compelling. Imagine how you might react when he opens with words like these:

> Blessed are the poor in spirit, for the kingdom of heaven is theirs.
> Blessed are those who mourn, for they will be comforted.
> Blessed are the humble, for they will inherit the earth.
> Blessed are those who hunger and thirst for righteousness, for they will be filled.
> Blessed are the merciful, for they will be shown mercy.
> Blessed are the pure in heart, for they will see God.
> Blessed are the peacemakers, for they will be called sons of God.
> Blessed are those who are persecuted because of righteousness, for the kingdom of heaven is theirs.
> You are blessed when they insult you and persecute you and falsely say every kind of evil against you because of me. Be glad and rejoice, because your reward is great in heaven. For that is how they persecuted the prophets who were before you. (Matthew 5:3–12).

This teacher seems to contradict every picture of righteousness you've ever seen. He goes on, talking about salt losing its saltiness, the city on a hill God's people ought to be, and the law being even more strict than we thought. Then he hits you with the big hammer: "unless your righteousness surpasses that of the scribes and Pharisees, you will never get into the kingdom of heaven" (Matthew 5:20).

This teacher has your attention!

Wisdom Leads to Repentance

Why are the beatitudes such a compelling opening to the Sermon on the Mount?

There's a feeling we get when we learn something that seems true but contradicts what we already believe, already love, or already do. Thoughts like "this doesn't add up," and "am I doing it all wrong?" run wild in our hearts We'll do almost anything to make the feeling go away. It isn't pleasant, but it's an important part of learning wisdom from the Bible.

Jesus' listeners at the Sermon on the Mount probably felt that way. Only after He led them to question their picture of righteousness were they ready for His rebukes of the Pharisees' teachings on anger, lust, divorce, oaths, revenge, money, prayer, worry, and true righteousness. Only then did He close by calling them authoritatively to follow His teachings instead. Why would Jesus structure His sermon this way?

Just before his record of the Sermon on the Mount, Matthew summarizes Jesus' preaching with the words, "repent, because the kingdom of heaven has come near" (Matthew 4:17). Here we see the goal of the Sermon on the Mount, and of all Jesus' preaching: to call us to repentance so that we can receive the kingdom of heaven. Repentance means re-aligning your entire intellect, emotions, and will around a new center. It turns full-scale to believe, love, and act differently than before.

> Repentance means re-aligning your entire intellect, emotions, and will around a new center

Jesus was calling his listeners to repent by abandoning the false picture of righteousness the Pharisees were selling them. They believed the Pharisees' teaching, prized their false picture of holiness, and tried to imitate it. Jesus called them to leave all of it and, instead, accept His teachings, seek His kingdom, and do what He says. That's repentance.

But before they could get there, they first had to go through the unpleasant experience of realizing they were doing it all wrong. That is why Jesus showed us what we were doing wrong before showing us how to do it right. Today's Bible teachers have to do the same thing: lead students to repentance by showing them how they're doing it wrong before showing them how to do it right.

THE NEED FOR WISDOM

Have you ever learned something new that seemed to contradict what you already knew, loved, or did? I can remember the day after I learned to count calories, looking at the white 140 on a red can of Coke®. I did the math. Three cans a week times fifty-two weeks in a year divided by 3,500 calories in a pound added six pounds a year to my body.

This did not square with how I saw reality. The drink I thought was fine, loved the taste of, and drank regularly really was bad for me! The feeling was so unpleasant that I felt forced to either reject the new information or change everything. Suddenly, Coke Zero® didn't taste so bad.

That unpleasant feeling has been researched thoroughly since the middle of the 20th Century. We've learned a few basic things about it that are consistent with common sense. When you learn something that conflicts with what you already hold true, you feel the conflict within yourself and will go to great lengths to make it go away. Usually, people either reject the new information unreasonably, find a way to ignore it, or change. Researchers have coined a term for the sensation: cognitive dissonance. Cognitive because it has to do with learning and dissonance because you want it to stop. It's like a Red Alert in our hearts, a warning we experience because we have a built-in desire to be wise. We want to be wise and see ourselves as wise, so we do not like realizing we are being foolish.

But secular researchers have run into a big problem: cognitive dissonance doesn't square with the theory of evolution. According to the theory of evolution, traits that don't help species survive or procreate slowly get worked out of the gene pool. But cognitive dissonance doesn't help us survive or procreate. If the theory of evolution were true, cognitive dissonance should have faded away long "millions and millions of years" ago. Yet the research plainly shows we still experience it regularly. Ironically, this is causing many researchers to experience some cognitive dissonance of their own.

But what secularism can't explain, the Bible has long made plain. We experience cognitive dissonance because we desire to be wise ... but we need to repent to get there. This is what Dr. Danny showed in his doctoral dissertation: that the Bible explains cognitive dissonance better than secular evolution does.

Positive Examples from Scripture

When we scan the Bible for times when someone changes what they believe, love, and do (someone who repents), we see an interesting pattern. Before changing to do it right, people first have to realize they are doing it wrong. This appears to be a consistent part of God's work changing our hearts. That is why the best teachers in the Bible, especially God himself, show people their wrongs before showing them what's right.

James 3:1–12 has moved many to seek the maturity in Christ that comes with a controlled tongue, to become "mature, able also to control the whole body" (James 3:2). James gets the attention of teachers like you and me early by triggering cognitive dissonance: "Not many should become teachers, my brothers, because you know that we will receive a stricter judgment." (James 3:1). An immature teacher, without control of his tongue, should read those words and tremble. He is engaging in activity that will bring stricter judgment upon himself, yet he doesn't have self-control! What he believes (Jesus' standard of righteousness), what he wants (to be judged faithful by Jesus), and what he is doing (teaching before reaching maturity) add up to conflict with this new information. He's feeling some very unpleasant cognitive dissonance.

Now he is ready to repent when James shows him how haphazard teaching can burn through a church (James 3:5–6) or guide the body astray (James 3:3–5). What's worse, he can't tame his own tongue (James 3:8)! This will drive him to repentance as he remembers that only true religion can tame his tongue (James 1:26). James uses the unpleasant alarm of cognitive dissonance to lead his readers to repentance. He introduces just enough new information to show them the error of their ways.

This pattern surfaces many times in Scripture — people experience inner conflict and see their need to change before they change. Most of the book of Job is filled with cognitive dissonance for both the reader and Job himself. His suffering, his righteousness, and God's righteousness do not add up. As the pages turn, the inner conflict Job and his readers experience mounts until God breaks it with His own words. Neither the reader nor Job would be ready to say "I repent in dust and ashes" without dozens of chapters full of cognitive dissonance (Job 42:6). Before God turns our lives right-side-up, He shows us how they are upside-down.

> Before God turns our lives right-side-up, He shows us how they are upside-down.

Negative Examples from Scripture

Sadly, cognitive dissonance doesn't always lead to repentance. When a wealthy young man asked Jesus how to inherit eternal life, Jesus wisely prompted cognitive dissonance within him. The young man wanted to please God and inherit eternal life, conflicting with his love for his wealth. Jesus had already taught that you can't love both God and money (Matthew 6:24). So, Jesus pointed out the contradiction by telling him "If you want to be perfect. . . go, sell your belongings and give to the poor, and you will have treasure in heaven. Then come, follow me" (Matthew 19:21). The young man's desire for eternal life and his love for wealth were not compatible. But he resolved the tension the wrong way: he went away sad (Matthew 19:22).

Most tragically, cognitive dissonance can also be used to manipulate with lies. Satan used this trick when he asked Eve, "Did God really say, 'You can't eat from any tree in the garden'?" (Genesis 3:1). When she misreported God's command, Satan assured her, "No! You will certainly not die … In fact, God knows that when you eat it your eyes will be opened and you will be like God, knowing good and evil" (Genesis 3:4–5).

Before hearing those words, Eve's world added up perfectly. But, once the serpent added new (false) information, things no longer held together. How could God say that? Would a good God keep Eve from becoming like Himself? Are His ways truly good? Eve (and Adam) resolved the dissonance in the most tragic way of all — by rebelling against God and eating from the forbidden tree. Satan's evil exploitation of cognitive dissonance led our first parents to make the wrong choice.

THE NEED AND THE TEACHER

Bible teachers, of course, want to see students change from wrong to right — not the other way around. So, we try to use cognitive dissonance to see our learners choose repentance and good fruit.

If regular repentance is part of following Jesus, all this means that Bible teachers need to show students their need for change before we show them the truth. Our students cannot afford to be wise in their own eyes.

> Cognitive dissonance can be exploited for bad or used for good

They must turn from evil, fear the Lord, and then grow in wisdom (Proverbs 3:7).

That is why the first question this book gives Bible teachers is "*WHY?*" It's probably the last thing you will determine in your lesson plan, but you should present it first. Students ask, even if they don't verbalize it, "Why do we need to learn what you're about to teach us?" If we can show them why, they're much more likely to listen to what teachers have to say. We will cover this more fully in the second section — *WHAT?: SEARCHING THE BIBLE* — but here are some examples.

If you're teaching from John 3:16, show first how the learners' lifestyles will lead to perishing. Then teach them, "For God loved the world in this way: He gave his one and only Son, so that everyone who believes in him will not perish but have eternal life."

If you're teaching from James 1:2–4, remind them first of the trials they can't make sense of. Then tell teach them, "Consider it a great joy, my brothers and sisters, whenever you experience various trials, because you know that the testing of your faith produces endurance. And let endurance have its full effect, so that you may be mature and complete, lacking nothing." Or you could show them how much they are going to need endurance to make it through the Christian life, and then let the passage tell them how God gives endurance to them. Either way, show them why they need it before you give it to them.

If you're teaching from Hebrews 11:1, show them first how badly we typically want to see something before we believe it. Then teach them, "Now faith is the reality of what is hoped for, the proof of what is not seen." You may also want to use other passages in the Bible to show that without faith no one will see the Kingdom of Heaven.

To help them embrace your teaching, show them first why they need it. What aspect of human life does your teaching speak to? How does it challenge what they already believe, love, and do (across all three learning domains)? Show them that contradiction! They'll probably feel some uncomfortable cognitive dissonance, but they're much more likely to pay attention, repent, and grow in wisdom.

Helping your students answer the Effective Four — *WHY?* • *WHAT?* • *SO WHAT?* • *SO WHAT NOW?* — will engage their built-in desire to be wise. They will want to be engaged with the information and then connect biblical truth to their lives. To be prepared, you have to study the Bible well. The next section in this book will help you do that.

Additional Resources for

The Importance of Bible Teaching

For More Study of the Wisdom in Proverbs

- Byargeon, Rick W. "The Structure and Significance of Prov 9:7–12," *Journal of the Evangelical Theological Society* 40 (1996): 367–75.
- Garrett, Duane A. *Proverbs, Ecclesiastes, Song of Songs*, The New American Commentary. Nashville: B&H, 1993.
- Murphy, Rowland E. *Proverbs*, Word Biblical Commentary. Dallas: Word, Inc, 2004.
- Waltke, Bruce K. *The Book of Proverbs, Chapters 1–15*, The New International Commentary on the Old Testament. Grand Rapids: William B. Eerdmans, 2004.

For More Study of Contemporary Writing on Affect

- Moody, Josh, and Robin Weekes. *Burning Hearts: Preaching to the Affections*. Ross-shire, Great Britain: Christian Focus Publications Ltd, 2004.
- Smith, James K. A. *Desiring the Kingdom (Cultural Liturgies): Worship, Worldview, and Cultural Formation*. Grand Rapids, MI: Baker Academic, 2009.

For More Study of the Homeostatic Drive for Wisdom

- Bowen, Danny R. "A Biblical-Theological Model of Cognitive Dissonance Theory: Relevance for Christian Educators." PhD diss., The Southern Baptist Theological Seminary, 2012.
- Festinger, Leon. *A Theory of Cognitive Dissonance*. Stanford, CA: Stanford University Press, 1957.
- Snapper, Marion. "Motivation for Learning Faith-Knowledge," in *Christian Approaches to Learning Theory: A Symposium,* ed. Norman De Jong. Lanham, MD: University Press of America, 1984.
- Sousa, David A. *How the Brain Learns*, 5th ed. Thousand Oaks, CA: Corwin Press, 2016.

SUMMARY:

THE EFFECTIVE FOUR QUESTIONS

The method outlined in this book revolves around four questions. If you look back at the table of contents, you will see that the book, itself, is laid out using these Effective Four — *WHY?* • *WHAT?* • *SO WHAT?* • *SO WHAT NOW?* (saying these with an emphasis on every other word — WHY what SO what SO what NOW — makes it easily memorizable.)

The questions are addressed in one order while preparing and presented in a different order while teaching. The rest of this book teaches you how to use these four questions to study a Bible text and turn it into a Bible lesson. Before we get there, it's worth it to familiarize yourself with each question:

IN YOUR STUDY
(FROM THE TEACHER'S POINT OF VIEW)

WHAT?: What is the truth of the passage I am going to teach? How confident am I that the truth I see is the truth that God and the human author want me to see? How can I give my learners confidence that this truth is God's truth?

So WHAT?: Knowing what I know about my learners, in what specific ways might this truth apply to their lives? How can I show them how this might fit or how it could change their lives for the better?

So WHAT NOW?: How can I get them to commit to at least one change from the possibilities covered? How can I build in accountability so that they will be more likely to follow through on that commitment?

WHY?: How can I show them that something in their lives doesn't align with the truth? Is there a recent event that shows the disconnect? Is there a believable hypothetical situation I could share that could help them feel like something doesn't fit? In other words, can I make them a bit uncomfortable without discouraging them?

IN YOUR LESSON

(FROM THE STUDENT'S POINT OF VIEW)

WHY?: Why do I need to know the truth you are going to teach? Give me a picture of what needs to be different. Where does the truth not align with other things in my life?

WHAT?: What is the truth that you can convince me exists in what you are teaching? Don't boggle my mind with too many details. Just show me the truth and how the biblical author makes his case for that truth.

SO WHAT?: How might that truth make more sense of my life? Or how might it change my life so that I am more like Christ in my home, my church, my workplace, my neighborhood, my recreation?

SO WHAT NOW?: What specific change should I commit to right now? Can you help me align my life to God's truth in at least one way today? Do you really care if I change?

What?
Searching the Bible

Hopefully you are convinced that heart changes need to be the primary, rather than the tertiary or, worse, neglected aim of your teaching. I have to admit that there are many examples of bad teachers manipulating affections to a desired end. That is not my purpose in writing. Instead, I want you to be able to apply biblical truth to the hearts of your learners so that they may be transformed into Christlikeness. To do that, you need the Bible, superintended in its writing, illumined understanding, and applied by the Holy Spirit.

There are many legitimate ways to study the Bible. But studying in order to teach it requires a special approach. You want to be confident that you understand the text before you attempt to teach your students. Then, you want to understand the best way to communicate the biblical truth to them before you call them to commit to transformation in their lives. This section goes through the process of discerning the truth of any biblical passage, long or short. That answers the first question of the preparation process: What does the text say?

The best way I have found to study the Bible is called inductive Bible study. This method not only allows me to understand the Bible so that I might be transformed by it; it allows me to understand the Bible so that those I teach might be transformed by it. Because inductive Bible study is so useful, it has become my go-to method for study regardless of my purpose in opening the scriptures.

4

What is the Bible?

Some may ask, "Why study the Bible at all?" The Bible makes its own best case:

> 2 Timothy 3:16 All Scripture is inspired by God, and is profitable for teaching, for rebuking, for correcting, for training in righteousness, ¹⁷so that the man of God may be complete, equipped for every good work.

Inspiration

The word inspired is a translation of a word that Paul uses that means "God-breathed." Scripture is God's very words written by men, but written in such a way — superintended by the Holy Spirit — that the words are actually the exact words God intended for us to have. Admittedly, we understand the process of inspiration no better than we understand how God could have spoken the world into existence;

> The words of Scripture are actually the exact words God intended for us to have

but we believe it anyway. Throughout history, men have tried to summarize their understanding in short confessions and creeds. These do not pretend to be inspired of God, but they do attempt to explain to ourselves and others what we mean.

> 1st Article of *The Westminster Confession of Faith*
> Although the light of nature, and the works of creation and providence do so far manifest the goodness, wisdom, and power of God, as to leave men unexcusable; yet are they not sufficient to give that knowledge of God, and of His will, which is necessary unto salvation. Therefore it pleased the Lord, at sundry times, and in divers manners, to reveal Himself, and to declare that His will unto His Church; and afterwards for the better preserving and propagating of the truth, and for the more sure establishment and comfort of the Church against the corruption of the flesh, and the malice of Satan and of the world, to commit the same wholly unto writing; which makes the Holy Scripture to be most necessary; those former ways of God's revealing His will unto His people being now ceased.

For example, the 17th Century Westminster Confession of Faith begins with a chapter on the Bible. In ten articles, the authors of this historic document summarize their understanding of Scripture. The first article introduces the Bible in language that is clear but archaic.

> **Article I: The Scriptures, *The Baptist Faith & Message* (2000)**
> The Holy Bible was written by men divinely inspired and is God's revelation of Himself to man. It is a perfect treasure of divine instruction. It has God for its author, salvation for its end, and truth, without any mixture of error, for its matter. Therefore, all Scripture is totally true and trustworthy. It reveals the principles by which God judges us, and therefore is, and will remain to the end of the world, the true center of Christian union, and the supreme standard by which all human conduct, creeds, and religious opinions should be tried. All Scripture is a testimony to Christ, who is Himself the focus of divine revelation.

The 2000 *Baptist Faith & Message* of the Southern Baptist Convention captures the same idea in a way that is easier to understand for modern English readers.

INERRANCY

In addition to inspiring the Bible, we believe that the Holy Spirit has preserved the Bible for us down through the ages. This is one reason we are able to teach the Bible. Although none of the original physical writings (autographs) have been preserved, the words they contained have been passed down to us so that what we have is the inerrant Word of God in written form just as He inspired it to be written long ago.

> What we have is the inerrant Word of God in written form just as He inspired it to be written long ago

In the last few decades there has been debate about what is meant by saying the Bible is inerrant. The best description I know of was crafted in 1978 by a group of evangelical leaders. The result of their work is a series of nineteen affirmations and denials along with a longer explanation of their understanding. Collectively, these are known as the *Chicago Statement on Biblical Inerrancy*. The document itself is easy to find on the internet. It is summarized in five short statements from the document.

> **A Short Statement, *The Chicago Statement on Biblical Inerrancy* (1978)**
> - God, who is Himself Truth and speaks truth only, has inspired Holy Scripture in order thereby to reveal Himself to lost mankind through Jesus Christ as Creator and Lord, Redeemer and Judge. Holy Scripture is God's witness to Himself.
> - Holy Scripture, being God's own Word, written by men prepared and superintended by His Spirit, is of infallible divine authority in all matters upon which it touches: it is to be believed, as God's instruction, in all that it affirms: obeyed, as God's command, in all that it requires; embraced, as God's pledge, in all that it promises.
> - The Holy Spirit, Scripture's divine Author, both authenticates it to us by His inward witness and opens our minds to understand its meaning.
> - Being wholly and verbally God-given, Scripture is without error or fault in all its teaching, no less in what it states about God's acts in creation, about the events of world history, and about its own literary origins under God, than in its witness to God's saving grace in individual lives.
> - The authority of Scripture is inescapably impaired if this total divine inerrancy is in any way limited or disregarded, or made relative to a view of truth contrary to the Bible's own; and such lapses bring serious loss to both the individual and the Church.

Authority

The last summary statement of the *Chicago Statement* mentions authority. Because the Bible is authored by God, we believe it carries His authority.

That authority has specific application. Take a look again at 2 Timothy 3:16–17 to see what profit Scripture is to us. It is good for teaching us what is true, for rebuking us when we believe (and teach) non-truth, for correcting us when we are unrighteous in our deeds, and for training us in how to live righteous lives. The Bible is God's authoritative book on what to know and what to do to be Christlike — "complete" is the term Paul uses. The purpose of being complete is being "equipped for every good work," what the Bible calls ministry.

> The Bible is God's authoritative book on what to know and what to do to be Christlike

Since it carries His authority, the Bible is sufficient for both knowing and knowing what to do. If God wanted us to know more, He would have inspired more words to be written. For example, He might have inspired the other letters Paul wrote to the Corinthian church so that we would have them in our Bibles.

Since God knows what He wants us to know and He knows us better than we know ourselves, we trust that He has given us what we need.

THE GRAND STORY

What we need most is to know God. And so, He reveals Himself in Scripture. One way He does that is to show us His grand story. Through that story, God shows us who He is. He reveals to us what it was like when He created the world. He reveals the consequences of the fall of humanity into sin. He reveals His plan of redemption that is first mentioned in Genesis 3:15, where God gives the first promise of Messiah, and is then worked out through the remainder of Scripture. He even gives us a glimpse of the consummation of history in the new creation and judgment of all humans with two, and only two, outcomes — eternal life or eternal death, that is, heaven or hell (see, for example, Matthew 25:31–46).

As we teach sections of Scripture, we need to remember to teach how the particular passage fits within that grand meta-narrative and how all our stories are rolled into God's grand story. Most of the Bible is written about the redemptive part of the story so, within the redemption story, we need to help learners place themselves relative to the major events of redemptive history so that application of the truth of the passage meets at least one of Paul's descriptions of the value of Scripture. We need to be careful not to misapply truths from one part to our learners who may be living in another part of redemptive history.

TRANSLATIONS

As I said before, the Bible is inerrant in the original writings. Those writings were in Hebrew, Aramaic, and Greek, none of which are understood by many today. Does that mean that we cannot actually know what God said? Far from it!

There have been English translations of Scripture for almost half a millennium. The beloved King James Version, also known as the Authorized Version, was an early translation into English for the Church of England that has been updated multiple times over the centuries. It remains one of the most popular translations of the Bible as well as one of the most popular books in print. There are other translations that vary based on the translation purpose, method, and source documents used by the individual or team that translated from the original languages. (Note: For deciding which translations to use, see the recommended resources at the end of this section.)

At one extreme, there is a translation method called formal equivalence that attempts to translate word-for-word from the original languages keeping the original word order as much as possible within the restrictions of English grammar. At the other extreme is a translation method called dynamic equivalence in which the translators try to bring into English the meaning of the phrases of the original languages without being limited to individual word choices. Between these are a number of translation methods that aim for something between these extremes.

From most of these translations, it is easy to understand what the original language writers meant to communicate. Where a single translation fails to give a clear understanding, examining two or three additional translations across the translation spectrum helps.

The bottom line is that you can rest easy; you do not have to become fluent in several languages to understand what God meant to say. The energy you save in translating you can spend on finding application of the truths evident in Scripture.

5

How to Study the Bible

In the introduction to the second section — *What?: Searching the Bible* — I admitted that my preferred method of Bible study is an inductive one. By inductive I mean that interpretation of biblical truth comes from looking at the biblical text. This way, observation comes before interpretation and interpretation comes before application.

This chapter walks through the steps of inductive study and gives an example using a study of 1 John 1:1–4. The worksheets that I use in the examples are available in the Resources & Helps section at the end of this book, with more freely available at www.TeachersOfTheBible.org. Feel free to use resources found there as you find them helpful.

Inductive Bible Study

Using an inductive method effectively means that you spend time in God's word before you open the commentaries, read the Bible introductions, or even glance at the notes in a study Bible. Understand what the Bible says and, from that, understand what the Bible means.

Observation

Yogi Berra once quipped, "You can observe a lot just by watching." That's the best way to start studying the Bible: just look at it. Read the passage several times from a single translation. Jot down notes on words, phrases, sentences, or explanations that don't seem clear. Listen to the passage read by someone else. Read the same passage from other, very different translations (See Translations in the previous chapter). Compare anything unclear from the®® passage to these translations. Do they make more sense? Contrast these translations with the original and with each other. Are there more questions that come to mind? If so, write them down so that you can find the answers later.

Who, if anyone, is mentioned in the passage? Are they doing something or is something happening to them? What is going on around them? Where in space and time does the author place the passage? Does the author answer the question why? If so, why *what*? Can you answer these questions from the passage or do you have to infer something that is not explicit? All of this is the beginning of observation.

Now that you have gotten familiar with the passage, try to figure out *how* the author is saying what he is saying. He is using words and phrases within the rules of grammar to communicate to his original audience. He is also using expressions of speech that would have been familiar to himself and the original audience. He is even unconsciously using his own personality in choosing how he communicates to his audience.

We are at a disadvantage compared to that original audience. We don't know the author like they might have known him. We don't live in their language or culture. We may not be familiar with their geography and what would have been current events in their world. What we do know is what the author wrote. We can see his words translated into our own language. And, as believers, we have the Holy Spirit, who superintended the original writing, illuminating the passage to our hearts and minds so that we can find the transformational truth of the passage. While supernatural, the Holy Spirit's work is not mystical; through His indwelling, He guides us as we examine the actual words written.

As you read, what words and phrases help you understand other words and phrases? Are there repeated words that seem to be emphasizing a certain point? Are there connecting words like "but," "to," and "therefore" that reveal how the author is making a main point and supporting it with details or examples? Is the author comparing or contrasting two things? Does the author connect some ideas with a timeline or a change in geography? Does he explain a truth and then apply that truth for his readers?

> **Observation Worksheet**
>
> Passage: *1 John 1:1–4*   Primary Translation: *CSB*
>
> Other Translations: *NASB / ESV / NLT*
>
> What words, phrases, sentences, or explanations seem unclear?
> - *Does "declare" refer to the entirety of 1 John or does it refer to something specific within the letter?*
> - *Is there a difference between "seen with our eyes" & "observed" in v. 1?*
> - *Who are "we"?*
>
> Are there additional questions that arise from comparing translations?
> - *Does declare (v. 3) modify the message (CSB = "we also declare to you"; ESV = "we proclaim also to you"); or the readers (NASB = "we proclaim to you also")?*
> - *Is the NLT correct in interpreting personal pronouns (him, he) where CSB, ESV, and NASB have relative pronouns (that which, what)?*
> - *Are the CSB and NLT correct in using "revealed" where the ESV and NASB talk about "manifest"?*
>
> What are the repeated words/phrases?
> - *We/our x 14*
> - *Sensory terms (heard, seen, touched) x 7*
> - *What/it x 7*
>
> What connecting words (e.g., but, to, therefore) does the author use?
> - *So that (verses 3 & 4)*
>
> Do there seem to be comparisons or contrasts?
> - *No comparisons or contrasts*
>
> Is there an apparent timeline or geographical progression?
> - *No progression except from John (& we) to his readers*
>
> Is there a truth with an application for the original readers?
> - *What John (and others included in "we") experienced with 3 of the primary senses (presumably Jesus, though not explicit)*
> - *The proclamation John is making has the purpose of fellowship with 2 persons of the Trinity as well as John (and others included in "we")*
>
> What type of writing (genre) is the passage (e.g., narrative, drama, discourse, parable, proverb, poem, prophecy, apocalypse)?
> - *1 John is labeled as an epistle (letter), but it doesn't begin with letter-like language seen in other NT letters (e.g., from, to, greeting)*

Structure

One of the simplest methods of determining what the author meant to say is laying out the structure of the passage. Though simple, this is not easy. After years of practicing, I still find it time-consuming to outline the passage using a structure that makes sense of the passage. There is no single way of doing this that works for everyone. What I try to do is get the big idea or ideas on the left side of a page. Without changing the order of the words, I move pieces of the passage to places on a page that make sense. I line up other parts of the passage under the words or phrases they seem to modify in some way. As I continue this process I end up with the finer details on the right.

This time spent in laying out the structure helps me later as I prepare the actual lesson. Because of time constraints, choices must be made on how much emphasis to give to any part of the passage. If I have very limited time to teach, I know I can only teach the big ideas from the left side of the page. The more time I have, the further I can get into the details in at least some of parts of the passage. If I wanted to make better JEOPARDY!® contestants, I could focus only on the right side of my outline. If, instead, I want to see transformation, I want to be sure to cover the big ideas on the left. Again, there is no magic method that you must use. Instead, do what you need to see how the words form the author's

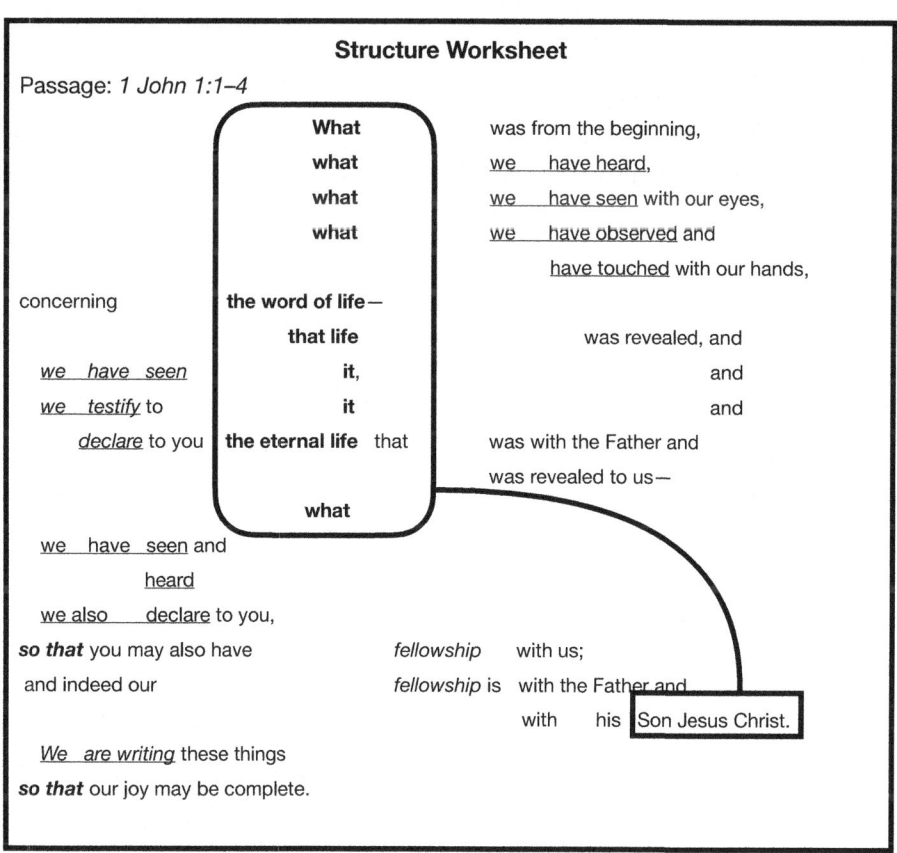

sentences, how those sentences form paragraphs, how the paragraphs form sections, and how those sections fit together to form the book.

Context

Once you begin to understand the passage you are studying, take a look on both sides of it. What do the sentences and paragraphs immediately before and after say? How does the passage you are going to teach fit in its immediate context? Not only are the words of Scripture inspired, the ordering of the sentences is superintended by the Holy Spirit. Try to understand what the author is saying in the wider context and determine how your passage is used to make his point. Why does the author include a word, phrase, or sentence? Why does he put it here instead of somewhere else?

Beyond the immediate context, take a look at the whole book from which the passage is drawn. What is the author's overall purpose? Where in the book does your passage come? Is it early in a Gospel so that it is introducing the characters that will have an increased tension throughout the narrative? Is it at the end of an epistle where the letter writer is telling his audience how to respond to the truths he communicated early in the letter? Is it the climax of a poem? Is it a detail that explains how a historical passage is progressing?

Even wider than the book, in which of the Testaments does the passage come? Is it before Christ's incarnation or after? In the New Testament, is it before the Holy Spirit's permanent indwelling of believers at Pentecost or after? In the Old Testament, is it before the exile of Judah into Babylon or after? The answers to all these questions can help you understand what the author meant to say to his original audience. Understanding what he meant to say is where we move from observation to interpretation.

WHAT? — SEARCHING THE BIBLE

Context Worksheet

Passage: *1 John 1:1–4*

How does the passage fit into the sentences and paragraphs immediately around the passage?
- *Opening verses so nothing before*
- *The next sections discuss fellowship in the light and the believers' advocate, Jesus Christ, making clearer the subject of "that which" in these verses.*

How does the passage fit into the book as a whole?
- *John contrasts true believers from pretend believers throughout the book. These opening verses make clear that John (and "we") are witnesses to the physical manifestation of Jesus.*
- *In 1 Jn 1:5, he gives details about the message he/they received from Christ.*
- *In 1 Jn 2:1, John describes the reality of sin and, in the following verses, what Christ does about it so that we can stay in fellowship with God.*
- *In the rest of ch. 2 and ch. 3, John describes fellowship between believers as evidence that they are in fellowship with God.*
- *In ch. 4 and 5, John applies a test to the evidence so that the believer can have assurance of salvation.*

How does the passage fit with the Testament in which it occurs?
- *The New Testament testifies to Jesus, the promised Messiah/Christ, who has come to save those who would have fellowship with God. The NT makes clear that Jesus came in the flesh, died in the flesh, and was resurrected in the flesh so that those who would accept His salvation have the same hope in being reconciled to God.*
- *Throughout the NT, there are challenges from both inside and outside the body of followers of Jesus. John seems to be describing a particular challenge from inside the church.*
- *This letter starts with "from the beginning," which is the same place he starts his Gospel. The description of Jesus seems to refer back to the Gospel of John (the beginning of Jesus' ministry) and forward to his book of Revelation (the completion of Jesus' ministry).*

Interpretation

Not only is where the passage occurs important, so is the type of literature, or genre, of the passage. Many modern authors have attempted to list the biblical genres and you can search the internet for the many divisions. Basically, there are narratives that describe facts, dramas that describe stories, discourses that describe topics, parables that describe truths, proverbs that describe truisms, poems that describe emotions, and prophetic and apocalyptic writings that describe things previously hidden. The bottom line is that each genre was written differently and thus has to be interpreted differently. We don't listen to a country song the same way we read the United States Constitution. Neither should we read the Psalms the same way we read Leviticus. Try to identify the style of writing and then read according to the way the passage was written.

At this point in your study, you should have a good sense for what the author meant to say to his original audience. That is the point of interpretation. The passage cannot mean to us what it never meant to them. Of course, we may have a deeper understanding of the truth communicated by the author because of progressive revelation wherein God gave to each age of history what the people who lived then needed to know. Now that the canon of Scripture — the 66 books of our Bible — is complete, we can understand more fully what God, as the ultimate author, meant to communicate even if the human author did not.

Speaking of the canon, take the truth you think you have discerned from the passage you are going to teach and test it against the whole counsel of God. Where else in the same book does the author write about the same truth? Did the author write any other books that may shed some light on his teaching? Are there other authors from the same Testament that discuss the same truth? How does the other Testament testify to the same truth. This process really relies on the overarching method of allowing Scripture to interpret Scripture. God is consistent in His truth so we can rely on the whole of Scripture to help us understand any single passage.

So, as you have studied a passage from Scripture alone, what do you think the passage meant to them? What did the author mean to communicate to his readers? That is the heart of the first question we ask in our preparation: What does the text say?

Sometimes, we aren't able to answer all the questions we wrote down in the observation phase of our study. Before finalizing your answer to the interpretation question, you may want to check some resources outside the Bible. That is the topic of the next chapter.

Interpretation Worksheet

Passage: *1 John 1:1–4*   **Genre:** *Letter? (possibly sermon)*

What is the big idea of this passage (e.g., what did it mean to the original readers/hearers)?

- *Jesus, the Word of life/the eternal life, is the source of fellowship and that fellowship completes the joy of John (and others? included in "we/our").*

Is this big idea explained elsewhere in Scripture? If so, what other passages either explain better or support your interpretation of this passage?

- *John is echoing the solution to our separation from God's fellowship because of sin. The solution is Jesus. John's explanation is clear enough here. The idea of fellowship with other believers is supported, in part, by the greatest two commandments — love God; love those who are made in God's image. Even more specifically, much of the NT is about fellowship in the church, built on the foundation of the apostles with the cornerstone of the foundation being Jesus.*

Moving outside the time of the original readers, what is the truth communicated in the big idea of this passage that is true across all time and in every place and culture?

- *The truth is transferable as-is. Jesus remains our only source of fellowship, which results in joy forward to his book of Revelation (the completion of Jesus' ministry).*

6

Resources for Studying the Bible

Finally, we have gotten to the place that many teachers mistakenly start, that is, in resources other than the Bible. Extra-biblical resources include Bible dictionaries, atlases, commentaries, concordances, and software. There are at least three legitimate reasons to open these resources. First, you may have unanswered questions remaining from the notes you took in the observation phase of your study. Second, you may want to explore further a topic that intrigues you. Third, you will want to check your work against experts in their fields of study. Essentially, these resources help you study the Bible with the help of the church by your side rather than on your own.

> **Legitimate Use of Extra-Biblical Resources**
> 1. Answer remaining questions
> 2. Explore a topic deeper
> 3. Validate interpretation of passage

Remember that your goal in interpretation is to understand what the author — divine or human — meant to communicate to his original audience — reader or hearer. If you think you have discovered a meaning never before uncovered, you are probably wrong! The Bible isn't saying anything today that it didn't say yesterday. Brilliant scholars have dedicated their lives to the study of the whole or the parts of Scripture. If you think you find the current head-of-state or particular current events referenced in God's Word, you are, more than likely, imposing something on the Bible. **Don't!** Let the Bible show you what was meant to be communicated and let the experts help you refine and gain confidence in your interpretation.

> If you think you have discovered a meaning never before uncovered, you are probably wrong!

Concordances

Perhaps you saw a word in the text that you don't understand. One way to solve your problem is to open a Bible concordance that shows every place in Scripture the same word appears. Examine these other passages to see if they make the word clearer. Be careful, though. Just as in English, the same word may have a variety of meanings ("semantic range" is the technical term) depending on how and where it is used. For example, in English, the word love may mean anything from a strong affection (as in "she loved her child") to a zero score in tennis (as in "the score is 30–Love"). Don't impose a meaning on the word in your passage just because it meant something

> Don't impose a meaning on the word in your passage just because it meant something somewhere else

---

Looking at my observation worksheet, I am interested in 3 terms
- *Declare: The specific word translated "declare" is used only in 1John 1:1–2 and Matthew 12:18.*
- *Seen (with our eyes): Of the 8 words translated into English as "seen," John uses 6 in his Gospel, these 3 epistles, and Revelation. 75% of the time, he uses the word as here.*
- *Observed: There are many words that are translated "look." At this point, the concordance does not seem helpful.*

Conclusion: *A Bible dictionary or commentary is going to be more helpful in understanding the scope of "declare."*

A Bible dictionary is likely going to be more helpful in understanding "seen" and "observed" since they are used widely.

---

somewhere else. It may or may not be the same meaning.

BIBLE DICTIONARIES

Another way to understand a word more fully is to look up the word in a Bible dictionary. Like any dictionary, the range of meanings can be found along with variations of the word. Some Bible dictionaries go one step further and identify what the modern author(s) believe to be the specific meaning of the word within each passage where it occurs. A word of caution is that these assignments of meaning to particular passages are not infallible; but they can be a help if you have done your work diligently before approaching the dictionary.

> Looking at my observation worksheet and the work from the concordance, I am still interested in 3 terms
> - *Declare: The specific word translated "declare" is used only in 1John 1:1-2 and Matthew 12:18. It has a sense of reporting or telling rather than declaring good news (as in Luke 4:18 and Revelation 14:6), commanding another to declare (as in Luke 9:60 and Romans 9:17), shouting/crying out (as in John 7:28), declaring publicly (as in Acts 13:24), or revealing (as in Ephesians 6:19).*
> - *Seen (with our eyes): Of the 8 words translated into English as "seen," John uses 6 in his Gospel, these 3 epistles, and Revelation. 75% of the time, he uses the word as here meaning seeing something that has become visible or has appeared rather than simply seeing something that Is (as in John 20:29, Revelation 1:19, or Revelation 16:15), observing (as in John 9:8), looking at/beholding (as in John 1:14, John 11:45, 1John 4:12, or 1John 4:14) or at the other extreme revealing or making clear (as in John 3:21).*
> - *Observed: This is another term for seeing that implies intentional looking/beholding.*
>
> **Conclusion:** *The use of the two terms for seeing seems to be an emphasis that John (& "we") are witnesses to the incarnate Jesus (which accounts for the many ways he describes having witnessed the incarnation — 3 of the 5 primary senses).*
>
> **Not yet answered:** *Still cannot tell if declaring (telling) is limited to something in the opening verses or if it refers to the entirety of the epistle*

BIBLE ATLASES

Some joke that the Bible is God's revelation "from Genesis to maps," trying to highlight the truth that God has revealed historical events that influence the maps we find at the back of many of our Bibles. An expanded set of maps is often published as a Bible atlas — maps with specific events, travel routes, and changing borders identified pictorially. These can help those of us unfamiliar with the geography and topography of the ancient world to place the events we read about in Scripture into their proper locations. For example, from looking at an atlas, it is easy to see how the nation of Israel was strategically placed at the crossroads of major trade routes of the ancient world that allowed the truth of God to go out into the whole world.

Sometimes examining an atlas raises necessary questions that we would not have from the text alone. For example, when we read that Jews in the Old Testament — and Jesus in the New Testament — "went up" to Jerusalem, a map shows that

Jerusalem is not north of the rest of Israel. That might move us to explore what the Bible means by "up." We in the West typically consider north as up. A Bible atlas might clarify that Jerusalem is actually at a higher elevation than some of the surrounding area, a different sort of "up."

> *John does not mention from where or to where he is writing. He seems to be familiar with the congregation(s) to which he is writing so it is possible that these are the same churches to which he addresses letters in Revelation at the command of Jesus.*
>
> **Conclusion:** *At this point, an atlas doesn't seem particularly helpful in interpreting this passage.*

COMMENTARIES

As valuable as concordances, dictionaries, and atlases are, commentaries are arguably the most relied-upon extra-biblical resources available to the teacher. Commentaries, and the authors behind them, can be our best friends or our worst enemies.

> Commentaries, and the authors behind them, can be our best friends or our worst enemies

They can be our best friends because they have already done much of the hard work described so far in observation and interpretation. Some even help us with the next phase of Bible study — application. If we don't know much about the author of a book of Bible, the commentaries help us not only identify, but understand something about the author. If we don't understand the historical events or the situation into which the author wrote, the commentaries can help. If we are unsure of the use of words or phrases, the commentaries reveal the commentators' understanding. If the style of a Hebrew poem or a First Century letter is as foreign as the language in which it was written, commentaries can get us up to speed. If the really hard work of outlining the passage to understand the structure of the author's method of communicating is too much, commentaries offer outlines for us. If we want to understand how the passage we are studying fits in its context and exemplifies its genre, there are the commentaries awaiting with possible explanations. With all this value, why not rely on these friends before starting our own work? Aren't we trying to "reinvent the wheel" when we do the work for ourselves?

No. These friends can easily become our enemies. How can that be? I can think of at least three ways.

First, like every translator of the Bible, every commentator approaches Scripture with a bias. That bias may be, for example, denominational, eschatological, or philosophical, but it is there. The author of a commentary usually communicates that bias even if differing views are presented in a detailed discussion of a book or passage. You may agree with the bias of the commentator and, so, be blind to it. You may disagree and, so, reject what would otherwise be sound reasoning and seek a friendly word from a different commentary. Either way, you may be tempted to give the commentator an inordinate amount of attention.

The second way that the commentaries can become enemies is along the same line — you may inadvertently place human authority over biblical authority. What the commentator writes may become your filter for understanding the biblical passage rather than your understanding of the Bible being the filter by which you read the commentaries. From personal experience, I can say this is an easy trap to fall into. The time of teaching is rapidly approaching. Life is happening all around. Suddenly, you find yourself relying on what the commentator wrote as you quickly read the passage you are about to teach.

Even if you disagree with the commentator's bias, the commentary can influence your reading of Scripture as you work as hard as you can to disprove the commentator's opinion. Either way, human authority is as tempting as the deceiver's promise in Genesis 3, "…you will be like God, knowing good and evil."

Commentaries can tempt us to sin in another way — they can make us lazy. Especially if I have found a commentator that I can rely on, I am tempted to avoid the hard work that is required in observing the biblical text before consulting any other source. My guess is that this is a frequent temptation for other teachers living busy lives. Note that my point is not to discourage use of commentaries; only to use them for the right reasons.

While there are literally hundreds of pages that can be written from a study of the introductions and commentaries, I try to focus on 3 things. First is answering unanswered questions from personal study in the Bible. Second is recognizing important or interesting information that did not occur to me to ask about in my own study. Third is to confirm my understanding of the text.

> **Answering questions:**
> - John's declaring is the entirety of his letter rather than something specific in the opening verses. It is proclamation rather than apologetics and theology (understanding of God) rather than ethics (understanding of right choices and behavior).
> - The use of two terms for seeing and looking upon are to emphasize that John and others were eyewitnesses. The "beloved apostle" John was formerly a disciple of John the Baptist and one of the first of the disciples Jesus called to Himself. By the latter years of John's life (likely date of letter), the church was growing in diversity and at risk for straying from the faith.
> The churches in the area of Ephesus (from which and to which he likely wrote) were made up of a mixture of people from backgrounds that would have made it difficult for them to believe either the full divinity of Jesus (Messiah) or the full humanity of Jesus. This is a building concern as some have gone out from the churches and have now returned as itinerant preachers with a different "truth." These may have been represented at the two extremes by pre-Gnostics of the day — Docetists, who doubted Jesus' humanity, teaching, instead, that He appeared to be human but didn't actually suffer pain and death on the cross, and Cerinthians, who doubted Jesus' divinity, teaching, instead, that Jesus was a human on whom "the Christ spirit" descended at His baptism and reascended just before the crucifixion.
> - "We" is debated. The evidence seems strong for this being either the apostles of Jesus or a larger group of disciples who were eyewitnesses to Jesus' earthly ministry. Some also make the argument that it includes the true church, which maintains an ongoing witness to Jesus.
>
> **Other important information:**
> - The genre is more likely a sermon than a formal letter. As such, it may have been read as a sermon to a variety of congregations.
> - The joy — abiding in Christ's love — may have been John's (& other witnesses') that would not have been complete as long as those for whom they had a responsibility were at risk for following false teachings. It may have also included the joy of the church as believers are unified with right doctrine.
> - More closely tied to 2 & 3 John, which is not that obvious on a first read. In 1 John, the author addresses those who would be influenced by the false teachers. If they are following in the ways of the false teachers, they need to be admonished along with the false teachers. If they are true believers they need to rest in the assurance of their salvation. In 2 John, the same author warns against helping these itinerant false preachers. By showing hospitality, they become guilty of supporting the false work. In 3 John, John discusses the other side of the issue: supporting true itinerant preachers by showing hospitality allows one to participate in true spread of the gospel.
>
> **Confirming my understanding:**
> - The book, itself, is probably more of a sermon than an epistle, despite the label applied.
> - This passage is a complete thought. That is, I have not artificially divided the text where it should not be divided.
> - The focus is on the person and work of Jesus, the Christ, against those who would teach falsely about either His divinity or His humanity. He is eternal life because He is divine and that life can be passed on to us because He is human.
> - The point is unity of fellowship with God and with other believers.

Software

In our age of technology, we have resources available that no generation before us had. Software (apps) make all the above resources accessible with just a click or two on our computers or smart phones. More powerfully, software often links the different resources in a way that uncovers the most helpful resources quickly. These have the same benefits and risks of the commentaries above but also present the temptations many times faster than physical books.

There are free, paid, and free with some paid resources available for your computer and/or smart phone. The field is ever-changing so reviewing current software has limited value in a printed resource. My suggestion is to develop a strong method for studying the Bible and then explore what (if any) software fits your purse, personality, and practice. The most expensive software available is worthless if you can't or won't use it well. Free software isn't free if it costs you more time than you can afford.

> I use software that allows incredibly fast research with supplemental resources tied to the biblical text. The upside is that I can resolve outstanding issues (see above) quickly. The downside is that I can be overwhelmed with information or I can be tempted to overwhelm my learners with too much information and risk losing the life-transforming truth I am responsible to communicate. In the case of my study of 1 John, I spent hours reviewing "interesting" information that has no place in the lesson. So, what you see in just over a page of notes is really a summary of many pages of notes collected.

Interpretation Refined

Hopefully you came to these extra-biblical resources after having a preliminary interpretation of the passage you plan to teach. Now that you have wisely used these resources to refine your understanding of the passage, it is time to decide what the original author meant to say to his original audience. Your initial assessment may have been spot on. If so, your work in the extra-biblical resources can give you greater confidence as you move forward.

If your view changed about what the passage meant, can you isolate the cause of the change? If it was a sound argument or additional facts that the biblical passage did not provide, you have used the resources wisely. If you have just come to rely on the commentator as a substitute for hard work, you have used the resources foolishly and you risk becoming a stumbling block for the learners you will teach. If that risk does not concern you, return to the study in Chapter 1 to refresh your humility.

The God we serve and His self-revelation in the Bible are worth our time and effort. Start with the Bible. Understand everything you can from your own study of God's word. Consult outside resources as necessary to answer questions raised during your study and to confirm your understanding of the passage.

Now, put into a single sentence the big idea of the passage you will teach. This is the clear answer to your first question: what does the text say? You can back up that big idea with a few details to remind yourself why that truth is true or how that truth may have moved those original readers or hearers, but it is important to refine your thoughts on what they were taught. Only then can you find in that truth the eternal truth that can be brought across the language and cultural differences, through the space and time changes to your modern learners — the subject of the next section of this book. If a reporter from a local news program interviewed you in your study time, what is the sound bite you would give them from the passage you are planning to teach? Would you share a cool fact or wow them with wisdom?

> Revised interpretation:
> *Jesus, the Word of life/the eternal life, is the source of fellowship and that fellowship completes the joy of the true church.*

Having worked hard to refine your understanding of a passage into a clear sentence, it is time to move from studying the past to studying your students in the present and planning for their transformation in the future. Those are the subjects of the next section.

Additional Resources for Searching the Bible

For More Study of the Nature of the Bible

- Erickson, Millard J., *Christian Theology*, 3rd ed. Grand Rapids, MI: Baker Academic, 2013.
- Grudem, Wayne. *Systematic Theology: An Introduction to Biblical Doctrine*, 2nd ed. Grand Rapids, MI: Zondervan, 2020.
- MacArthur, John, and Richard Mayhue. *Biblical Doctrine: A Systematic Summary of Bible Truth*. Wheaton, IL: Crossway, 2017.

For More Study of Translations of the Bible

- Bible Versions and Translations https://www.biblestudytools.com/bible-versions/
- Fee, Gordon D., and Mark L. Strauss. *How to Choose a Translation for All Its Worth*. Grand Rapids, MI: Zondervan, 2007.

For More Study of Interpretation of the Bible

- Fuhr, Richard Alan Jr. *Inductive Bible Study: Observation, Interpretation, and Application Through the Lenses of History, Literature, and Theology*. Nashville, TN: B&H Academic, 2016.
- Kaiser Jr., Walter C. and Moisés Silva. *Introduction to Biblical Hermeneutics: The Search for Meaning*. Grand Rapids: Zondervan, 2007.
- Klein, William W. and Craig L. Blomberg and Robert L. Hubbard Jr. *Introduction to Biblical Interpretation*, 3rd ed. Grand Rapids: Zondervan, 2017.
- Köstenberger, Andreas J. and Richard Patterson. *Invitation to Biblical Interpretation: Exploring the Hermeneutical Triad of History, Literature, and Theology* (Invitation to Theological Studies Series), 2nd ed. Grand Rapids: Kregel, 2021.
- Plummer, Robert and Benjamin Merkle. *40 Questions About Interpreting the Bible* (40 Questions & Answers Series), 2nd ed. Grand Rapids, MI: Kregel, 2021.
- Carson, D.A. *Exegetical Fallacies*, 2nd ed. Grand Rapids, MI: Baker Academic, 1996.
- Zuck, Roy B. *Basic Bible Interpretation: A Practical Guide to Discovering Biblical Truth*. Colorado Springs, CO: Cook Communications Ministry, 1991.

To Find More Supplemental Resources

- Carson, D.A. *New Testament Commentary Survey*, 7th ed. Grand Rapids, MI: Baker Academic, 2013.
- Glynn, John (editor). *Best Bible Books: New Testament Resources*. Grand Rapids, MI: Kregel Ministry, 2018.
- Glynn, John. *Commentary & Reference Survey: A Comprehensive Guide to Biblical and Theological Resources*. Grand Rapids, MI: Kregel Academic & Professional, 2013.
- Longman, Tremper, III. *Old Testament Commentary Survey*, 5th ed. Grand Rapids, MI: Baker Academic, 2013.

So What?
Making It Matter

Everything up to this point has been about discovering the truth from the Bible. That truth can be applied to any learner. You could use the work up to this point to teach anyone anywhere.

Now we move to work specific to you students. Your specific learners will need to have that truth communicated in a way that they can understand and that matters to their unique lives. So, the work from this point forward will change depending on what you know about them. The next three chapters should help you know your learners, adapt the truth from Scripture for them, and aim for transformation in them.

7

KNOWING YOUR LEARNERS: PART 1

Because of the fall, the way your students see themselves is never 100% clear. You can serve as their spiritual optometrist to help them see themselves more accurately as they learn to compare themselves to the truths of God's word. In their comparison, they should see their need for the Savior.

> You can serve as your learners' spiritual optometrist to help them see themselves more accurately as they learn to compare themselves to the truths of God's word

As spiritual optometrists, we serve a repeated, though temporary, role. As their sight changes over time, we help learners adjust their prescription so that they see more clearly in a wider field of view. But, again, this is temporary. The good news is that a permanent solution is available. We can help them see more clearly for now, but the Holy Spirit can do corrective surgery so that they do not need corrective lenses. Of course, that work will not be perfected until glorification in the new creation. Until then, He calls and equips teachers to help disciples of Jesus to see themselves more clearly and to desire transformation that only He can provide.

A word of caution. As the teacher, you can divert their attention away from their needs by having them focus on you rather than compare themselves to Scripture. This happens anytime you become the object of the lesson instead of the biblical truth you found in the passage. You can impress them with the time you spent preparing. You can wow them with the facts you gleaned in your study. You can fool them with your false fluency in foreign languages. Any of these risks distracting them from the real focus of the transforming truth in the Bible.

Better, you can take a position that allows them to focus on the truth of God's word, the reality of their distortion from what they are called to be, and, so, help them be transformed. To do that effectively, you must know what they need and know something about how they learn in order to meet that need.

What They Need Ultimately

Ultimately, what your students need is to be conformed to the image of Christ. The entire person is affected by the fall so that everything is, at least partially, out of alignment. This brokenness shows itself differently in each person, and each of us were made unique to begin with.

> Ultimately, what your students need is to be conformed to the image of Christ

This chapter asks what we can learn about our unique students before we consider how to answer the *So What?* question. Before we consider what we can learn about our students, let's review some earlier concepts.

While considering the whole person, teachers can aim for changes in the three learning domains — cognition, affection, and behavior as described in Chapter 2 and as demonstrated in Chapter 9.

Scripture makes clear that, as the center of affections and volition — desires and decisions — the heart is the center of motivation for the person. Jesus explains why the heart is key in Luke 6:43–45.

> Luke 6:43 A good tree doesn't produce bad fruit; on the other hand, a bad tree doesn't produce good fruit. 44 For each tree is known by its own fruit. Figs aren't gathered from thornbushes, or grapes picked from a bramble bush. 45 A good person produces good out of the good stored up in his heart. An evil person produces evil out of the evil stored up in his heart, for his mouth speaks from the overflow of the heart.

So, as explained in Chapter 2, our lessons need to begin with our aim at seeing their hearts conformed to Christ. But we must also consider the cognitive domain, their knowledge, their minds. Paul makes this challenge in Romans 12:2.

> Romans 12:2 Do not be conformed to this age, but be transformed by the renewing of your mind, so that you may discern what is the good, pleasing, and perfect will of God.

The result of both affection and cognition is behavior. Behavior set perfect is perfect obedience to God's design. In John 14:15, Jesus taught that love for Him would be demonstrated.

> John 14:15 If you love me, you will keep my commands.

In Chapter 1, the Great Commission was connected to all three of these learning domains. There, the discussion was focused on the teacher. But the point of teaching is to make disciples who would reach and teach additional disciples, so the learning domains set right — *orthodoxy, orthopathy, orthopraxy* — are for teacher and learner alike. Setting these right will result in wisdom, that is, rightly relating to God, self, others, and all of creation.

WHAT THEY NEED IMMEDIATELY

To help your students grow in Christlikeness, you must show them how properly to live in each of these relationships throughout all spheres of their lives. Show them how wisdom results in a right relationship with God. Begin with a proper "fear of the Lord" described in Chapter 2.

Show how that results in:
- ▶ hearing from God from His self-revelation — Scripture.
- ▶ talking to God through prayer.
- ▶ approaching God through the advocacy of the Son, Jesus.
- ▶ walking with God in fellowship through the indwelling of the Holy Spirit.

Then, show them how wisdom results in a right relationship with themselves, having neither too high a view of themselves because they are fallen creatures nor too low a view of themselves because they are made in the image and likeness of God, unique among all of creation.

Rightly relating to God and self, they can then rightly relate to other people, again thinking neither too highly nor too lowly of those made in God's image — none of your learners is God, but all are made in the image and likeness of God.

Wisdom even extends to all creation, which Paul describes in Romans 8:22 as "groaning together" because of the effects of the fall of humanity into sin. Show your learners how that, while the trees and spotted owls do not deserve preference over humanity, care for the earth and the plants and animals that inhabit it are part of our stewardship of the good gifts of God.

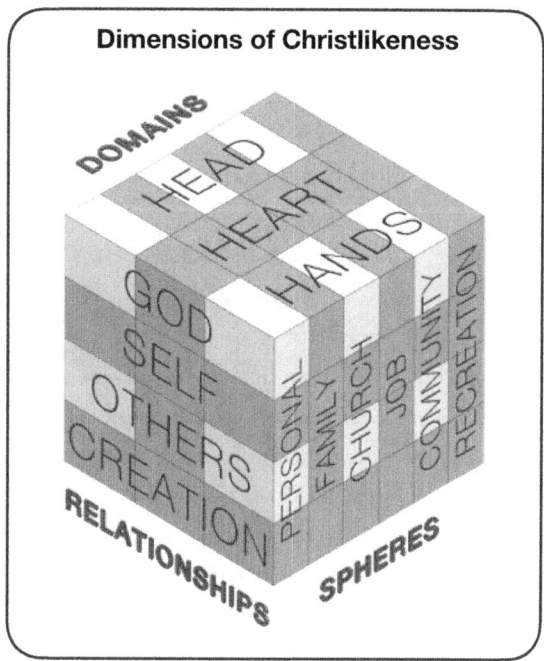

In summary, help your learners know how to function in Christlikeness in their homes, in their churches, in their jobs, in their communities, and in their recreation. Show them how each relationship in each sphere of their lives may help them grow in Christlikeness in head, heart, and hands — the 3 learning domains.

Depending on how well you know your learners, you can tailor your lesson to their needs addressed in the passage you will teach. If you don't know them at all — for example, if you are a guest teacher at a state-wide meeting — you still know something about them because you share their general needs. If you know them intimately because you have been in relationship with them for years, you can address more specific needs.

As you prepare your lesson, pray that the Holy Spirit would move you to address the most pressing needs that He is aware of, whether or not He makes those needs known to you. It has happened often that I have prepared a lesson for a specific group of learners and something from the lesson — even something that I considered a secondary point to the lesson or something that I was certain I explained poorly — has touched the lives of some

> Pray while you are preparing the lesson that the Holy Spirit would both superintend your preparation and prepare the hearts of your learners for the lesson He has superintended

of my learners in ways that I could not have anticipated. Pray while you are preparing the lesson that the Holy Spirit would both superintend your preparation and prepare the hearts of your learners for the lesson He has superintended. This is a prayer He is willing to answer in the affirmative every time since this is why He has called and equipped you to teach.

How They Learn

Knowing the needs of your learners, you now need to know how they learn. Before getting to them, let me ask about you. How do you think you prefer to learn? The answer may not be as simple as you think because the question is not as simple as you might think. To get a clue how you prefer to learn consider how you typically teach. Do you usually lecture? Lead a discussion? Divide your learners into small groups to work through case studies? For most teachers who know nothing of learning styles, their preferred method of learning is also their default method of teaching. They are often unaware they are created differently from at least some of their students. Sure, they know that some people are naturally drawn to their class while others prefer the teaching style of another, but most teachers attribute those choices to compatibility of personalities rather than learning preferences.

Several authors who write about learning styles rely on the work of David A. Kolb, who described a learning cycle that each of us goes through as we learn and learn to apply what we have learned. This cycle includes a range of ways of taking in information and then a range of ways of processing the information taken in.

Taking in New Information

To gain new information that may lead to wisdom, the learner can either experience it or think about it as the information is presented.

Experiencing new information typically begins with the primary senses — seeing, hearing, touching, tasting, smelling. Each learner prefers some senses over others and, as the teacher, you need to consider those whose preferences are different from yours. For example, if you always lecture, those who prefer to take in information through the sense of hearing will be engaged; others may not. If you always have the learners read something for themselves, those who prefer to hear may be less engaged. For those who prefer the sense of touch, if you do not sometimes offer hands-on instruction, they may never be moved.

For learners who prefer to gain new information by thinking, if you rush through the content that you are trying to teach, they may not have time to consider what you want them to learn. For this type of learner, even a "take 2 minutes to consider…" approach gives them time to take in the new information so that they can learn. Assigning pre-class work ("homework") may help these learners engage during the time in class.

Almost all learners use some combination of experiencing and thinking, but the balance of the two is unique to each learner. For example, to understand how Christ sees the lost immigrant poor of our community, the learner may experience the work of the Holy Spirit during an outreach event to clothe and house the poor and come to realize that each is made in God's image and deserving of dignity, respect, and the gospel. At the other extreme, the learner may consider passages of Scripture that command caring for the foreigner and the poor and, from that study, gain an understanding of Christ's love for the lost. The combination of these two teaching methods will touch both learners.

Processing New Information

Once new information is taken in, the learner must process it in order to achieve wisdom from the biblical truth. Like gaining new information, this can be active or reflective. That is, the learner can actively experiment with the new information or can quietly reflect on that information, in effect, experimenting with it in the mind. Using the example from before, once the learner has achieved more Christlikeness in considering the poor immigrant, that information can be applied to real-life. For those who prefer active experimentation, they may choose to join or start an English-as-a-Second-Language (ESL) ministry or may fill backpacks for weekend provision for students in a local school. For more reflective learners, they may consider the many ways their church could reach the poor immigrants and then write a ministry plan for carrying out the best of those ideas. Learners at both ends of each of the ranges — information intake and information processing — can grow in wisdom within their own learning preferences. But how can the teacher teach such a wide range of learners?

Learning Preferences Simplified

The answer is as simple as the Effective Four. As another adaptation of Kolb's work, the Effective Four questions — **WHY?** • **WHAT?** • **SO WHAT?** • **SO WHAT NOW?** — at the center of the teaching model described in this book help the teacher prepare and then teach across each of the learning preferences. While every learner must answer all these questions to gain wisdom, the fact that each learner is unique can be a blessing and a curse.

> The fact that each learner is unique can be a blessing and a curse

It is a blessing in that preparing for the Effective Four, the teacher is making good use of our built-in need for relationships in the group of learners who form the learning community. The teacher can rely on learners with different preferences to be engaged more actively with the lesson at different points. Then, as a learning community, the class benefits from the preferences of each member of the group. For example, those who prefer the **WHAT?** can learn how to apply the new information from those who prefer to think about **SO WHAT?** Those who like to jump to action with the **SO WHAT NOW?** can be drawn into the lesson by those who help the group answer **WHY?** the group should consider the content of the lesson at all. Even the teacher's least preferred questions can be answered within a learning community if learners from each learning style are engaged.

As much of a blessing as learning preferences within the learning cycle can be, they are also somewhat of a curse. The teacher must consider teaching methods outside his or her comfort zone. The teacher must then attempt to teach to each learning preference so that every learner in the community is engaged with the lesson. If all are to gain wisdom, each must be engaged.

The curse of this diversity points to the real strength in the teaching method of this book. As long as the Effective Four — **WHY?** • **WHAT?** • **SO WHAT?** • **SO WHAT NOW?** — are planned for and answered as a result of the learning experience, each learner can be touched by the truth of God's word. But how can the teacher help the learners find application for real-life? That is the subject of the next chapter.

8

KNOWING YOUR LEARNERS: PART 2

From the inductive Bible study done in the second section — *WHAT?: SEARCHING THE BIBLE* — you can have confidence in understanding the truth the author intended to communicate to his original audience. From your interpretation, revised by your work from sources outside the biblical text, you have a timeless truth that is not limited to language or culture. From the study of your learners, you have a good idea what they need and how they prefer to learn. Now, it's time to consider how you are going to help them deduce application for their lives. This is the second question to ask when preparing, *SO WHAT?*

The first step is combining all this work into the actual point of your lesson. Without losing the truth of the passage, how can you communicate that truth in a way that your learners can actually be transformed by it? Remember that to understand the passage, you had to consider the time, culture, language, and even geography of

> Without losing the truth of the passage, how can you communicate that truth in a way that your learners can actually be transformed by it?

the original writer and reader. Now that you are nearing lesson preparation, you have to consider the time, culture, language, and geography of your learners. In addition to these, you need to filter the truth through physical and spiritual maturity lenses. Before we ask directly the *SO WHAT?* question, let's look at a few more factors to remember about our students.

TIME

A lot changed in the 400 years between the closing of the Old Testament and the opening of the New Testament. In our age of technology, life may be changing even more quickly today. Teachers must take this into account when we consider the lives of our students. The speed of communication is faster than it has ever been in the world. News that at one time would have taken months to reach other parts of the world — if even then — now travels at the speed of light.

This ultra-fast communication puts an overwhelming amount of information in front of our students. No one has time to read the nearly 63 million results that just came up (in 0.44 seconds) when I searched the internet for "Bible teaching." The astute teacher must remember how easy it is to be overwhelmed and then to overwhelm students with such technology and information in our time.

> The astute teacher must remember how easy it is to be overwhelmed and then to overwhelm students

Times will probably change more between our writing this book and you reading it. So, we'll have to leave it to you to ask: what is it like for your students to live in these times?

CULTURE

Not only have the times changed, the culture in which we live is considerably different from that/those of biblical times. Where you teach, the attitudes, customs, and common beliefs are probably different than they are where we teach. Even where you are, cultures vary from one group to another, from distinct people groups to local business offices.

While teachers and learners may have much in common, with our mobile society, it is more likely than ever that there are cultural barriers, seen or unseen. You may need to adjust a lesson for an urban, suburban, or rural learner. A lesson on justice is heard differently across ethnic boundaries.

Although, in Christ, the church is united, we remain a diverse people. Each element that comprises culture needs to be part of the culture filter through which the teacher passes the necessary truth so that it becomes an applicable truth.

LANGUAGE

Language is another filter that is used by the Bible teacher wishing to make learners wise. Apart from the inability of most of us to become fluent in any of the ancient languages represented in Scripture, there are at least three ways that language needs to be filtered by the teacher.

The first has to do with the native language abilities of the learner. A five-year-old can comprehend truth but not at the same level or with the same terms as the typical adult. Filter your language so that it matches the learner's ability. If you want to introduce terms that are beyond the learner, include an explanation in simpler terms.

The second is closely related. Adults cannot necessarily comprehend the same terms because of their education levels, natural language abilities, and native languages. For example, in the same class may be a believer who is a recent immigrant from a non-English speaking country, another believer who dropped out of school at a young age and never read anything but trade magazines and technical books, and a believer who is a seminary professor fluent in the shorthand theological terms bandied about at the school. The teacher must filter for all three. As with the first filter above, you may need to include explanations in simple terms as you use terms that may be beyond your learners.

The third filter is the difference in range of meanings of words from two different languages. For example, there are three words in New Testament Greek translated as the English word "love." Each of those words has a range of meanings that can be over- or under-emphasized by the unskilled teacher. They can be under-emphasized when reading John 15:17, where Jesus commands His followers to love one another using one of the Greek words for love, and two verses later He talks about the conditions under which the world would love His followers using another Greek term. He is talking about two different kinds of love and it is easy to miss the point in English because we have one word. The range of meanings can also be over-emphasized as in John 21:15–17 when Jesus asked if Peter loved Jesus. Jesus twice asked using one of the words for love and then the third time asked using the same word that Peter used to answer all three questions. The fact that there is overlap in the range of meanings of each of the Greek words for love means too much can be made when the teacher makes an emphatic declaration that competent translators disagree on.

This all sounds very complicated, but there is one simple solution: listen to your learners talk. You don't have to imitate them, but you do need to be aware of what words and phrases they understand easily.

Geography

Even geography must be filtered. If you teach in a flat, Midwestern state and you read about mountains in the Bible, do your learners envision the Rocky Mountains of Colorado or the foothills of the Appalachians in Kentucky? Does the interpretation change if you are teaching in Colorado or Kentucky? If Moses went up the mountain to receive the commandments of the Lord, did he ascend 1,000 or 17,000 feet? The geography with which the learner is familiar will become the interpreter if you, the teacher, are not.

Take a look at the maps in the back of your Bible or take a look at a Bible atlas. It should be immediately apparent that the maps have changed over the millennia. The world in which we live is dramatically different from the world of the Bible. The countries have changed. The cities have changed. Depending on the importance to the truth of the passage being taught, geography may need to be filtered depending on the geography of the learner.

Physical Maturity

People grow and change over time—from embryos to babies to toddlers to young to middle aged to elderly. Physically, we grow rapidly to a point and then start falling apart because of the effects of Genesis 3. Our brains are able to soak in information differently at different ages.

Though all age at the same rate, not all learners grow at the same rate. Some are able to handle complex information early; others much later; still others never. Attention spans differ by developmental age. Up to a point in later childhood, the average attention span in minutes is equal to the child's age in years. That is, a 2-year-old can pay attention to one thing for 2 minutes; a 10-year-old for 10 minutes. Adults, in theory, can pay attention much longer, assuming they do not have a screen in their hand!

Along with the physical growth comes some degree of maturity. As we learn more, experience more, fail and succeed more, we gain a knowledge base that allows us the opportunity to function more rightly within the created world. Wisdom is the term used when the opportunity is taken. Unfortunately, again because of Genesis 3, we often choose to be the fool rather than the sage.

> Because of Genesis 3, we often choose to be the fool rather than the sage

Physical maturity is a filter through which the truth of God's Word must pass if we are to teach our learners to be wise. The same truth can be taught to the 2-year-old, the 20-year-old, and the 90-year-old, but the truth has to be filtered for their different developmental maturity.

Spiritual Maturity

Many assume, wrongly, that physical maturity can be a good predictor of spiritual maturity. Instead, spiritual maturity really depends on if and when that learner was called from death to life (regenerated, in Christian terms) and how committed the learner is to growth in Christlikeness through the sanctification process.

One learner may use all the right terms, know all the right answers, and serve the church often — but still not be a true follower of Christ. In some ways, their knowledge can be a hindrance to transformation because knowledge puffs up. He and others around him "know" that he is okay.

Another learner may be growing quickly because she was called out of terrible sin as a late teen and has been feasting on the bread of life day-in and day-out for several years.

Yet another may have come to faith very late in life and has had no time to grow.

The point is that it is easy to assume and difficult to assess spiritual maturity. Only through a close relationship can you come close to knowing the specifics for each individual learner. Even with imperfect knowledge, spiritual maturity must be a filter through which you pass the biblical truth so that it can transform each learner in your class.

Considering what you know about them, you can begin to communicate biblical truth in a way that each learner can be transformed into Christlikeness. Aiming for that change is the subject of the next chapter.

9

Transforming Your Learners

So, who are your learners? Where do they come from ethnically, culturally, geographically? Where are they right now? What is their range of physical maturity? Spiritual maturity? Where are they going from here? Do you have another chance to teach them or are either you or they moving on? How do they prefer to learn? The previous two chapters have helped you think through these questions. With the answers, you are ready to answer the *So What?* question and determine the teaching point(s) of your lesson.

John Stott is credited with answering the question, "How many points should a sermon have?" His answer: "At least one." The same holds true for every Bible lesson; you should have a point. The point should be easily discerned by your learners. Don't make them work hard to understand your point; they will have to work hard enough to be transformed by it.

> Don't make your learners work hard to understand your point; they will have to work hard enough to be transformed by it

The main point of your lesson comes from the work you did in the second section — *What?: Searching the Bible* — where you took an initial interpretation of the Bible passage and revised it based on work you did from outside resources. Now it's time to adapt that truth to your learners and then develop learning aims for the time you have with them in the passage you will study together.

Teaching Point

According to 2 Timothy 3:16–17, Scripture is profitable for four things — teaching, rebuking, correcting, and training in righteousness. The first two address the head, teaching right beliefs about reality (a.k.a. doctrine) and rebuking wrong beliefs. The second

> 2 Timothy 3:16 All Scripture is inspired by God and is profitable for teaching, for rebuking, for correcting, for training in righteousness, 17 so that the man of God may be complete, equipped for every good work.

two address the hands, correcting wrong behavior and training for righteous behavior. In short, Scripture is profitable for making a person Christ-like.

Obviously, desiring these changes toward Christlikeness and committing to righteousness is a heart issue. That is why Chapter 2 is devoted to the heart of the matter — the heart. The Holy Spirit can change their hearts so that they do want to think righteously and to behave righteously. Then, when they think and behave like Christ, their hearts are even more like His.

Considering how Scripture testifies to its own application, your job is merely to communicate the truth of Scripture in a way your modern learners can understand so they might apply it to their lives. This is where your teaching point comes in.

The truth you saw after all your study may be directly transferable as your teaching point. You may have to simplify it if your audience is young. You may want to practice a bit of wordsmithing to make it more memorable, but don't change the truth presented. For example, my revised interpretation of 1 John 1:1–4 was "Jesus, the Word of life/the Eternal Life, is the source of fellowship and that fellowship completes the joy of the true church." To make that memorable for adults, I modified the order and the terms slightly to "Real joy comes from real fellowship with the real Jesus."

> Revised interpretation:
> *Jesus, the Word of life/the eternal life, is the source of fellowship and that fellowship completes the joy of the true church.*
>
> Teaching Point:
> *Real joy comes from real fellowship with the real Jesus.*

That teaching point needs to be stated word-for-word near the beginning of the lesson, at the end of the lesson, and, if the lesson extends for more than a few minutes, another time or two in the middle of the lesson. The idea is to get your teaching point across to your learners and repetition can be an effective way to do that. Remember this is not a mystery novel with the truth revealed at the end. This is a lesson meant to transform each of your learners. The sooner in the lesson they see the truth, the more likely they will remember.

Obviously, you must then show them how you came to that truth from the passage. Before that, you need to draw them into the lesson and, later, show them how that truth applies to their lives. But the idea here is to craft a teaching point that is short and clear enough to be remembered even if the details are lost from their memories. With that truth and the text before them, they may be able to reconstruct the support used as they reflect on the passage in the future.

> Craft a teaching point that is short and clear enough to be remembered

LEARNING AIMS

With the truth of the passage clear, you are ready to consider the learning aims of the lesson. Let me admit that, behind the difficult structural work done in Chapter 5, writing lesson aims seems to be the hardest part of lesson preparation for most teachers. I have been teaching in the church for more than three decades and have been structuring passages and writing lesson aims for more than a decade and I still find these time-consuming and difficult. But, let me emphasize that the work done in these difficult tasks pays huge dividends when you see learners transformed.

So, how do you want your learners to be transformed as a result of the lesson? Let's look at aims in each of the learning domains.

Affective Aim

Because the primary aim should be transformation of the heart (see Chapter 2), it is time to determine your affective aim. Let me reiterate that it is the Holy Spirit who will transform their hearts, but He has called and equipped you to be used in that process. He can help you as you prepare the lesson. He can prepare the hearts of your learners to receive and apply the truths He inspired to be written. Your responsibility is to be obedient to your calling and to do the hard work necessary to help your learners be transformed by Him.

Considering the truth of the passage, what desires, loves, or affections are likely to be changed? From those new or modified affections, what decisions or commitments should your learners be prepared to make?

So What? — Making it Matter

Take a look at my affective aim for a group of adult learners from 1 John 1:1–4: "The learner will desire real joy as a member of Christ's body." Notice that it is written in terms of the individual learner. It is not what I will do — for example, "I will show them how to have joy." It is not a general statement of hope — for example, "I hope that my learners will have a new heart." It is specific and it comes from the truth of the passage.

> **Affective (Heart) Aim:**
> *The learner will desire real joy as a member of Christ's body.*

As I said before, though, this aim is not measurable. How could you read the hearts of your learners so that you know you have achieved your aim? The short answer is that you can't. You have to trust the Holy Spirit to make this change but you can still aim to have the change in each learner.

What do they need to know and what do they need to do in order to experience and to demonstrate that change of heart? That is where the cognitive (head) and behavioral (hands) aims come in.

Cognitive Aim

What do they need to know? Well, they need to know the truth of the passage. If they understand the truth there, they are set up for change of the heart. To understand the truth of the passage, they may need to go through an abbreviated form of all or part of the inductive Bible study you did in preparing the lesson. They may need to see the structure of the passage in order to understand the logic of the original author. They may need to know about words or phrases used by the author to make his point. They may need to see the same truth emphasized elsewhere in Scripture. They may need to know other details you gleaned from outside resources you used in Chapter 5. What information is presented and how that information is presented is the subject of the fourth section of this book — *So What Now?: Turning It into a Lesson.*

Instead of committing to a method, at this point you need to aim at something to be learned in order that the heart change is likely. What is the central support the author provides for the truth he communicates? Finding that can help as you consider writing the cognitive aim.

From all the work on 1 John 1:1–4, it appears John is going almost to extremes to describe Jesus as both God and man. This supports the dual purpose of the book to admonish false teachers who have new teachings about Jesus and to assure true believers that the old teachings are still true — Jesus, the God-man, is the only means of being reconciled to God and Christ's body, the church. So, in this short passage, I really need two cognitive aims: one about the person of Jesus and one about the fellowship that comes from a relationship with Jesus.

> Cognitive (Head) Aims:
> - *The learner will be able to describe the support John uses in testifying about the person of Jesus.*
> - *The learner will understand the extensive fellowship that can be experienced with Jesus.*

Again, notice that the aims are written in terms of the learner rather than the teacher. The aims are not what we will do as teachers; they are the result of what we will do with our learners.

Also notice that, unlike the affective aim, which is not directly observable or measurable, both cognitive aims are measurable. There are several ways you can determine if these aims were met. You could give a short quiz either at the end of the lesson or at another class session. You could ask learners to call out answers to questions instead of giving a written exam. You could structure the lesson so that as they work through the text, they discover the answers. For example, in the ***WHAT?*** section of the lesson, you could prompt them to describe all the ways John uses to testify about Jesus, let them read the passage for themselves, and then discuss the responses. You could also tell them there is an extensive fellowship that John describes and ask them to identify the different relationships in the text [e.g., John and the reader, John and the Father, John and the Son, the Father and the Son, by extension, the reader and the Father and the Son].

Behavioral Aim

Knowing these facts (cognitive aims) and desiring the joy that comes from experiencing the truth of these facts (affective aim), you want to go one step further and aim for changes in what the learner will do to experience that joy (behavioral aim).

So What? — Making it Matter

This will be where your study of your learners plays a huge part. What might change in any of the spheres of their lives — personal, family, church, job, community, recreation — in any of their relationships — God, self, others, creation — within any of the domains — head, heart, hands? The list of possibilities is so large it shouldn't be hard to come up with examples. As you prepare, some will come to mind. Prioritize these and at least consider a couple of likely changes.

In the study of 1 John 1:1–4, the fellowship described transfers immediately to all the relationships in their lives and it is easy to see how fellowship might change in any of the spheres of their lives.

Not quite as obvious, the desire for joy may even translate into change in any of the domains of learning. For example, to experience the joy that comes from the fellowship with Jesus and His body, the church, they may choose to pay attention, in further study of 1 John (head), to the differences between the focus on admonishing the false teachers and those who would follow them and assuring the true believers that their faith is not in vain. They may choose to change their affections (heart) for irritating members of the church by praying for and by choosing to act kindly toward them. They may seek reconciliation with God if they are not yet Christ-followers or they may choose to intensify that fellowship through the practice of spiritual disciplines (hands).

As I have written the lesson on 1 John 1–4, it could be a single lesson taught to a large group that I may never see again. So, my behavioral aim is twofold: I want them to commit to reading the entire letter/sermon several times and, as they read, I want them to read themselves into the correct passages so that the nonbeliever does not find false assurance nor does the true believer find doubt.

> **Behavioral (Hands) Aims:**
> - *The learner will read through the book of 1John a dozen times in the next year.*
> - *The redeemed learner will experience joy by reading himself/herself into the assurance passages in 1John.*
> - *The unsaved learner will experience joy by accepting Jesus and the fellowship with God and the church He offers.*

S.M.A.R.T. Learning Aims

Again, coming up with the learning aims is one of the hardest parts of preparing transformative lessons. Along with structuring the passage (see Chapter 5), this is where I see teachers struggling the most. These are difficult enough that many teachers give them a miss. If you spend the time at least considering these two parts of the lesson preparation, your learners are more likely to be transformed by the lesson because you are more intentional in your effort.

Your learning aims need to be S.M.A.R.T. and connected. There are several variations of the S.M.A.R.T. approach to writing aims or goals. The version I recommend is adapted to transformative Bible teaching: **S**imple, **M**easurable, **A**chievable, **R**esults-focused, **T**imely.

Simple

Each aim should be simple. That does not mean easy. Simple means that each aim has a single focus. If the aim can be divided into two or more individual aims, it should be. That way you can explain to yourself and others what you are really trying to accomplish with each aim. You can also determine if you are trying to do too much in the time allotted for the lesson.

Measurable

The cognitive and behavioral aims should be directly measurable. For example, for the cognitive aim, you could go so far as give a quiz at the end of the lesson to decide how well the learners grasped the content of the lesson. More realistically, you could ask a question or two along the way (or even at the beginning of the next lesson) to measure their level of comprehension. For the behavioral aim, you might have them demonstrate some new or improved skill. For both, the measurability can be directly connected to accountability. Measurability is not as easy for affective aims since they cannot be measured directly. There is no meter that measures changed desires or decisions. Instead, when writing affective aims, determine what changes in cognition and behavior might be evidences of a changed affect. These indirect measures can then be used to help you discern transformation in your learners.

Achievable

Can the aim be reached in the span of the lesson or course for which it is written? If not, refine it. "The learner will be Christ-like" is not achievable in this lifetime, much less in a single lesson. The point of teaching for wisdom is to see the learner become more Christlike, but the aim of a single lesson needs to be more specific. For example, in what specific way or in what specific context could the learner be more Christ-like?

Results-Focused

The aim should be the result of the lesson rather than the method of teaching the lesson. For example, "The learner will study the extensive fellowship described in 1 John 1:1–4" is the method by which the results-focused aim rather than the goal. "The learner will understand the extensive fellowship that can be experienced with Jesus" is a goal that can be reached. The second aim can guide the lesson toward transformation while the first merely describes one of the methods that might be employed to accomplish the real aim.

Timely

The timeless truth of the passage being taught should be timely in its transformation. Is the aim relevant to the world in which your learners live? Is it appropriate for this stage of their physical and spiritual maturity? Will it apply to their lives as soon as the lesson time has ended? If the answer to each of these questions is "yes," then the aim is timely.

CONNECTED LEARNING AIMS

The aims for the lesson should not only be S.M.A.R.T., they should be connected. As you identify your learning aims, you need to make sure they are connected to the central truth of the passage, the real needs of the learner, and the other learning aims.

Connected to the Central Truth of the Passage

Does the aim apply the transformative truth of the passage to the individual learner's life? It should. You may have secondary aims that help the learner understand the support of the central truth, but don't get caught up in minutia and neglect the main point of the passage. If you find yourself over-achieving in your lesson aims, that is, if you have so many aims that they cannot all be achieved in the time allotted, favor aims connected to the central truth.

Connected to the Real Needs of the Learner

That means that the aim should be learner-centered. Even if you don't write the aim with this pattern, your determining the aim should complete the following sentence: "As a result of this lesson, the learner will…" So, this is not what you will do in the lesson. It is not even what the learner will do to reach the aim. It is transformation you want to see in the learner. How will he or she be different in thinking, desiring, deciding, or doing? The aims will help you determine what method you might use to see the transformation, but the method is not the end goal. Aim for the transformative end.

Connected to the Other Learning Aims

Each of the aims should be connected to the others. As discussed, educators divide the individual into domains of learning — cognitive, affective, behavioral — but you are trying to see transformation of a whole, an integrated, a psycho-spiritual unity, in short, a person. Each of the domains contributes to change in the others. What you know changes what you desire and decide; it changes what you do. What you desire and decide changes what you will know — or seek to know — and what you do. What you do changes both what you know — through the experience itself — and what you desire and decide.

This all sounds very intellectual, so let me explain using a real example. Imagine a person who struggles with some besetting sin that does not characterize your life. That knowledge changes your emotions about and your actions toward that person. How can you be transformed?

Well, it could start in the cognitive domain — your thinking. When you study Genesis 1–3 and come to understand how they have marred the image of God differently than you, your love for them changes because you recognize them as another image-bearer of God, which, in-turn, changes your behavior toward them. So, cognition changes affect, which changes behavior.

What if your affect changed first? For example, what if you shared some circumstances that made you have a new love or respect for them? That affective change will still result in behavioral changes, but it also changes what you know and what you seek to know about them and about God's truth. Affection changes both cognition and behavior.

What happens when you pray for someone? That simple behavior changes your knowledge of God's will and your love for God and His image-bearers. Behavior can affect the other two domains.

Since we are holistic beings, it shouldn't surprise us that each part of us affects each other part. Write your lesson aims so that they are as connected as the holistic person you are trying to see transformed.

My recommendation is to come back to this section periodically. Writing lessons aims is difficult. These tips should transform the transformative nature of your aims. Changing your aims will change your lessons. Changing your lessons will change your learners.

CONNECTING THE MODEL AND THE AIMS

The Effective Four help you think through your aims. **WHY?** do you want your learners to receive this lesson? That is your affective/heart aim — the transformation of the heart that should come with engaging with God's truth. **WHAT?** do you want them to know in order to have that transformation? That is your cognitive/head aim. **SO WHAT?** might they do as a result of this change of heart? **SO WHAT NOW?** will you call them to do? These last two combine to form your behavioral aim. Unfortunately, this part of the lesson is often neglected.

As described early in the book, an ineffective model has been passed down through generations of teachers of the Bible so that we often never get past **WHAT?** Please don't stop before you get these last two questions answered. The way to prepare and deliver a lesson in order to address each of the Effective Four is the subject of the next section of this book.

Additional Resources for

Making it Matter

For More Study of Learning Styles and Modalities
- Kolb, David A. *Experiential Learning: Experience as the Source of Learning and Development,* 2nd ed. Upper Saddle River, NJ: Pearson Education, 2015.
- LeFever, Marlene D. *Learning Styles: Reaching Everyone God Gave You.* Colorado Springs, CO: David C. Cook, 2004.
- Richards, Lawrence O., and Gary J. Bredfeldt. *Creative Bible Teaching*, Rev. & Upd. Chicago, IL: Moody Publishers, 2020.

For More Study of Learning Aims
- Anderson, Lorin W., and David R. Krathwohl, Peter W. Airasian, Kathleen A. Cruikshank, Richard E. Mayer, Paul R. Pintrich, James Raths, and Merlin C. Wittrock (eds.). *A Taxonomy for Learning, Teaching, and Assessing: A Revision of Bloom's Taxonomy of Educational Objectives.* New York: Longman, 2001.
- Bloom, Benjamin S. (ed.). *Taxonomy of Educational Objectives: Book 1 — Cognitive Domain.* New York: Longman, 1956.
- Bloom, Benjamin S. (ed.). *Taxonomy of Educational Objectives: Book 2 — Affective Domain.* New York: Longman, 1964.
- Pierce, Walter D. and Charles E. Gray. *Teaching in the Three Domains of Learning: The Taxonomies Simplified for Educational Objectives, Activities and Outcomes.* CreateSpace Independent Publishing Platform, 2013.

For More Study of the Learner
- Yount, William R. *Created to Learn: A Christian Teacher's Introduction to Educational Psychology*, 2nd ed. Nashville, TN: B&H, 2010.

For More Study of Application
- Mark Dever's Sermon Application Grid
  https://anglicanexpositor.files.wordpress.com/2011/10/application-grid.pdf

So What Now?

Turning It into a Lesson

By this point, you should know what transformation you are looking forward to seeing the Holy Spirit accomplish in your learners. You've answered all four questions: *WHY?* • *WHAT?* • *SO WHAT?* • *SO WHAT NOW?*

How do you turn that preparation into an actual Bible lesson? What will you plan to do in the classroom so that they will be engaged with the lesson and be transformed by Scripture? How do you know if you are making a difference in their lives? What can you do to continuously improve your teaching so that you are used more effectively by the Holy Spirit to transform those He indwells? Those are the questions answered in this section of the book.

10

Helping Learners Answer the Effective Four

Now it's time to plan to accomplish the aims you decided on in Chapter 9 so that you can get your teaching point from Scripture into the lives of your learners. In Chapter 7, I described the learning cycle and the value of the Effective Four questions — *Why?* • *What?* • *So What?* • *So What Now?* Let's see how to actually construct a lesson based on those questions.

Why Not *Why?* First?

As you prepare, it is natural to approach the questions in order. Don't! You can't discern why your students need to know what the text says of you don't yet know what the text says. If you start with *Why?*, you risk imposing your opinions on the biblical text.

I have seen and, embarrassingly, I have committed this error. It usually begins with a great illustration or case study you want to share with your class. Then, you start twisting the truth of Scripture to fit your illustration. You may not stray far from the text, but your main point didn't come from the Bible's main point. You want your learners to be moved by the illustration, so you aim for some form of behavior modification as you conform them to the illustration and then you send them out having learned a lesson straight from the shallow well of your wisdom.

The Order of the Effective Four

This may be the most difficult part of the method to understand: you don't prepare the questions in the same order that you present them. When preparing, the *What?* question comes first. But when teaching, the *Why?* question comes first. Here's what the order looks like.

The Order

Lesson Preparation	Lesson Delivery
	Why?
What?	*What?*
So What?	*So What?*
So What Now?	*So What Now?*
Why?	

So, begin your lesson preparation as described in the second section — **WHAT?: SEARCHING THE BIBLE**. When the answer gives you your teaching point, prepare the **So WHAT?** part of your lesson. Then, come up with a way to encourage them to commit to transformation in the **So WHAT NOW?** Only then do you go back and develop your **WHY?** The **WHY?** needs to raise an issue or surface a need that is finally satisfied by **So WHAT NOW?** This way, students are first motivated to change, then shown the truth behind the change, encouraged to consider possible changes, and then commit to at least one change, however small. That's not the order you prepared it, but it's the order in which their hearts will best receive it.

It might surprise you that we are not seeking dramatic change in every learner every time we gather — "going for the fence" in baseball terms. There are instances of dramatic change — regeneration to name the big one — but the usual aim should be consistent change — "single base hits" to follow the baseball analogy. If you can see small transformation lesson after lesson, you will see more and more Christ in them over time (see Chapter 12 for a measure of that change).

So, the teaching model itself is as simple as the Effective Four — **WHY?** • **WHAT?** • **So WHAT?** • **So WHAT NOW?** You prepare them slightly out of order and then deliver the lesson to them in this order.

Of course, if your lesson has more than a single point, you may want to have multiple combinations of **WHAT?** and **So WHAT?** That is, you may want to draw them into the lesson with the **WHY?** Then show them the **WHAT?** of your first teaching point. Cover the **So WHAT?** of that point. Show them the **WHAT?** of your second point. Cover the **So WHAT?** of that second point, etc., until you finally get them to commit to at least one point of transformation in the **So WHAT NOW?** But the pattern of the Effective Four remains **WHY?** • **WHAT?** • **So WHAT?** • **So WHAT NOW?**

THE MODEL MODELED

For the work I have been doing on 1 John 1:1–4, I have planned a 7–10-minute lecture (see next pages) that could be used as a one-off lesson or could be the introduction to a teaching series on 1 John. Whether or not your default teaching method is lecture, you need to consider the options described in the next chapter.

Passage: *1John 1:1–4*

Special Needs of Learners:
- *Mixed ethnicities, most Anglo*
- *Mixed suburban and rural*
- *Wide age range: 20s – 80s*
- *Wide range of spiritual maturity, not directly corresponding to physical maturity*
- *Most primary English; couple of ESL*

Aims:

Affective:
- *The learner will desire real joy as a member of Christ's body.*

Cognitive:
- *The learner will be able to describe the support John uses in testifying about the person of Jesus.*
- *The learner will understand the extensive fellowship that can be experienced with Jesus.*

Behavioral:
The learner will read through the book of 1John a dozen times in the next year. The redeemed learner will experience joy by reading himself/herself into the assurance passages in 1John.

The unsaved learner will experience joy by accepting Jesus and the fellowship with God and the church He offers.

Classroom Setup: *No special setup since this will be a short lecture-style lesson*

Passage: *1John 1:1–4*

Teaching Idea: *Real joy comes from real fellowship with the real Jesus*

Why?: *Why can't Christians just get along? I have heard preached that all we need to do is love Jesus and love others who call themselves Christians because doctrine doesn't matter. In fact, some say doctrine divides.*

Tx: *Doctrine was dividing the churches to whom the Apostle John sent his letters, but not because true doctrine divides. Rather, it was because false doctrine had to divide from sound doctrine — darkness had to remove itself from light.*

John wrote the sermon we know as 1 John probably to the churches in Asia Minor that included the 7 churches to whom he wrote at Jesus' request in the opening chapters of Revelation and possibly to the same audience he addressed the Gospel that bears his name. Some, who had been part of those congregations, had separated from the churches with new teachings about Jesus. Some denied His humanity. Others denied His divinity. All denied something about the truth that had been proclaimed to them.

John wrote to admonish those false teachers and to encourage the true believers. In the opening verses of 1 John, he shows that real joy comes from real fellowship with the real Jesus.

So What Now? — Turning it into a Lesson

What?:

1 Jn 1:1 Subject: Word of life, Jesus
Using the primary senses, John says in every way, he and his companions are witnesses to the work of Life incarnate

1 Jn 1:2 As an apostolic witness, John must testify to the eternal life incarnate.

1 Jn 1:3a As an obedient disciple, John must proclaim the truth he knows.

For this reason...
1Jn 1:3b The fellowship we enjoy with Christians is part of the fellowship we enjoy with God. We have been reconciled to Him and we have been put into the one body of Christ.

With this result...
1 Jn 1:4 Fellowship with God and with other true believers brings joy.

So What?:

Perhaps you don't experience that joy. That may because you are not one of God's children even though you would label yourself as Christian. Perhaps you believe, and maybe teach, contrary to the truth. If that's you, you need to read John's letter and hear the admonition John gives to the false teachers. Then, repent and turn to Jesus, who is the source of real fellowship with God and with God's people. Don't read yourself into the encouraging passages; they are not written to you if you are not a true child of God.

So What? (cont.):

Perhaps you are a new believer and the deceiver is trying to convince you that your salvation is not real. You haven't really changed, not enough that God would love you. If that's you, you need to read John's letter and hear the encouragement for those who are true Christians. Don't read yourself into the passages where John admonishes the false believers; that is no longer you.

Perhaps you are a maturing believer with some doubt. Some of the arguments made against sound doctrine make sense to you so that you wonder if you really are His. Like the new believer, you need to read John's letter and hear the encouragement for true Christians.

So What Now?:

If you are an average reader, you can read 1 John in about 10 minutes. Would you commit 4 hours over this next year to reading through 1 John 12 times and then meditating on its truth for 10 minutes after each read?

You should see that Christians can get along, but only if we agree on the core doctrines of the faith. John addresses one of those in the opening verses: Jesus is 100% God and 100% man. Any variation from that truth divides.

As you read and meditate, see how you can experience real joy that comes from real fellowship with the real Jesus that John introduces in these first 4 verses and fleshes out in the remaining chapters.

11

Teaching Methods

In Chapter 7, I introduced you to the idea that each person learns in a unique way. I also observed that, for most of us, our default teaching method is based on our preferred way to learn. Although we can think of groups of people preferring one of the Effective Four — *Why?* • *What?* • *So What?* • *So What Now?* — more than the others, every person you teach is at least slightly different from you. You will have to be intentional if you are going to reach all your learners. This chapter presents some of the popular teaching methods that can be applied to your entire lesson or to a specific part of the lesson.

Methods Appropriate for the Whole Lesson

There are at least three solid methods of teaching the whole lesson — lecture, discussion, and case-study. Let's take a look at how.

Lecture

The entire lesson can be done in a lecture. This is particularly appropriate for large groups but may be useful when time is very tight and you need to control the direction of thought. In a lecture, you will need to do more work to help your learners answer the Effective Four. You can draw them in with a good story, illustration, current event, or anything else that would create in them a desire to see an answer from Scripture. You can transition to the passage and teach them what they need. But then you come to the hardest part — you need to present the application (*So What?*) in a variety of ways so that each learner is able to draw an application out of the truth. Then you can challenge them to commit to transformation as you resolve any tension set up in the opening.

The strongest argument for the lecture method is the central teaching event of the church each week — the sermon. An expositional sermon is the most effective way healthy churches teach the congregation as a whole.

The strongest argument against the lecture method also comes from the pulpit. I have sat in churches and listened to winsome talks from pastors who occasionally cite Scripture in support of moralistic teaching from the latest popular book. Entertainment is not transformation. If someone in the audience were allowed to ask "*So What?*," the emptiness of the method would be evident to all.

In some circles, the lecture teaching method has been considered ineffective. As I hear the method applied and talk to others with strong feelings about lecture, I conclude that it is the lecturer, not the lecture method, that is more often the problem just as the pastor, rather than the sermonic method, is at fault for ineffective Bible preaching. A lecture done poorly does not engage the learners and, because unengaged learners become inactive listeners, their minds can wander to thinking about beating the Methodists (or Baptists or Presbyterians...) to the restaurant for lunch. On the other hand, a lecture done well can keep everyone moving through the entire learning cycle and can be used by the Holy Spirit to transform each one.

If you are going to use lecture, do it with excellence.

Discussion

The entire lesson can be built around discussion. With the right questions, you can facilitate a discussion that relies on the learners to fill in the details of the lesson. Assuming that some, if not all, of the learners in the class are regenerate Christ-followers, this method uses the community of believers assembled by the Holy Spirit to equip one another.

Discussion was my preferred method for years. It began with my sense of inadequacy of Bible knowledge and with my fear of hurting people by imposing what I saw in Scripture on others. What was derived from my weaknesses became a strength in my teaching and learners were transformed. I found that the key to leading a discussion was having the right questions.

The right questions can draw learners into the lesson by challenging inconsistencies in their beliefs that are evident, especially in extreme cases. For example, you may get them to agree that every person needs to hear the gospel so that they have the opportunity to respond by repenting of their sins and turning to Christ for salvation. Then present them with a worse-case scenario where they have the opportunity to witness to someone guilty of heinous crimes against humanity — Adolf Hitler, Saddam Hussein, Osama bin Laden, a local child-molester or serial murderer — someone they think deserves eternal punishment in hell. Ask if they would share the gospel with that person while praying that they would receive Christ. Then, lead them into a study of Jonah who didn't want to preach because the Ninevites might respond positively to the message and be saved (see Jonah 4:2 for Jonah's reasoning).

As you work through the passage of Scripture, you can ask questions that help your learners see the truth, the teaching point of the lesson. Then ask *So What?* What could that truth mean for their lives today, this week, this year? And, finally, ask how they would commit to living out that truth and be accountable to someone else in the group for living it out. All this can be done with the right prompts, the right questions.

The biggest drawbacks to the discussion method are time and direction. It takes more time to prepare a discussion than to prepare a lecture. You are never sure going into the classroom what issues may arise, what answers may be provided, what heresies may crop up. So, you need to prepare for several eventualities. You need to know the passage so well that you can stay in the truth even in the face of strong opposition from one or more learners. You need to consider how you would respond to likely challenges or perspective differences. You need to also be able to say, "I don't know; let me come back with an answer." That is a humbling response, but a very handy one when you get to places in the discussion for which you are not prepared.

On the other hand, discussion can exploit the strengths and learning preferences of every learner in the room. For each of the Effective Four — *Why?* • *What?* • *So What?* • *So What Now?* — you can enlist the learners who prefer that question.

If you are going to use discussion, do it with excellence.

Case-Study

Case-study is another method that can be used for the entire lesson. You can begin by presenting in word, print, or video clip a situation — real or hypothetical — that resembles an issue in the lives of your learners. Then as you walk through the case-study, you help them ask and answer the Effective Four from the passage of Scripture that holds the answer. A word of caution: Don't manipulate the truth of the passage to fit the case-study. If the Bible passage, as written, doesn't have the answer for that case, choose another case-study or choose another passage. Done poorly, this method risks turning Scripture into a self-help book. Done well, a case-study engages the learners in a safe way to walk through a tough problem.

> If you are going to use case-study, do it with excellence.

At this point, you might think this admonition has become trite, or at least tiresome. My point is that the Lord we serve is worthy of our best effort. Half-hearted preparation and teaching causes others think teachers have a half-hearted love for the Lord. You have an important role to play in being used by the Holy Spirit to transform the bride of Christ. Put your best effort into this and God will be glorified.

METHODS APPROPRIATE FOR PARTS OF THE LESSON

In addition to these, and other possible methods of constructing an entire lesson, there are specific methods that can be used for parts of the lesson. Your imagination is the limiting factor in using them; my imagination is the limiting factor in presenting them. Here are a few ideas to stir your imagination.

WHY?

To help answer this first of the Effective Four, you want your learners to be drawn to the biblical text for a specific purpose. How you raise the need that is satisfied by Scripture can vary lesson-to-lesson.

You could start with a **discussion** about a question that will not be fully answered until the end of the study. Allow, or even prompt, contradictory views if you use discussion to draw them in. The discussion can occur as a large group, within smaller buzz groups, or between neighbors, depending on the comfort level of your learners in any of these groupings. Some may say to one other person what they would not dare say in a large group. Be sensitive to what you know about your learners. Discussions in smaller groups can be brought back to the large group in the form of a quick reporting from each group, reporting of "best answers" from select groups, or by leaving the responses within the smaller groups until later in the lesson.

You could also use a **case-study** to raise their awareness of a need. Instead of using the case-study for the entire lesson, you could introduce it in the *WHY?* section and then return to it later in the lesson.

In addition to modifying these whole-lesson methods, you could use an **illustration**, a **story**, or a **video clip**, all with the same purpose as the case-study.

One way to use them is to set up a safe way to discuss an issue in the classroom. You make it safe by temporarily removing the learner from the situation. Instead of directly challenging the learner, together you are outsiders looking in on a situation — real or imagined — and exploring it abstractly before applying it to the real life of the learner.

Nathan demonstrated the safety of this method in talking to David about David's sin with Bathsheba recorded in 2 Samuel 12. Nathan presented a story of a wealthy man who had grossly wronged a poor man. When David responded with an appropriate judgment against the rich man, Nathan announced, "You are the man." What would have likely resulted in defensiveness from David instead resulted in repentance. Don't use this method every lesson or your learners will catch on and the method will become ineffective because they will already anticipate your turning the tables on them.

Any of these can be used in less dramatic ways. Remember that the point is not the illustration or story; the point is that you want your learners to understand there is a need to approach the biblical text you intend to teach. The method needs to be chosen, not for the impressiveness of the illustration, but for the value of God's Word that will meet a need for transformation.

You can also draw them into the lesson by setting up the tension with a short **debate**. You can have individuals or groups argue each side of an issue without resolving the debate until later. Using this method, you need to set it up so that the debaters are not necessarily in agreement with the point they are debating. In

So What Now? — Turning it into a Lesson

fact, it is sometimes helpful to have a person argue from a view with which they disagree to help raise the tension that needs to be resolved, in effect, forcing the learner to view something outside his or her own bias. Be sure that this is done without causing division in the church. The idea is to draw out the problem rather than drawing battle lines in the group.

WHAT?

To show them the truth in the passage, you could **lecture** on part or the whole of the passage, showing them the truth that answers the questions raised in some other way in the *WHY?*

Discussion is another potential method with one strong word of caution — do not turn discussion of the passage into opinion of the passage. That is, don't ask, "Susie, what does this passage mean to you? Tommy, what does it mean to you?" There is a truth in the passage because it is God's inerrant word. You have discovered that truth in your study. Ask questions and guide the discussion so they might discover the same truth.

You could also walk them through a shortened version of the **inductive Bible study** you did in preparing the lesson. This could include any step of the inductive Bible study that you found particularly helpful in understanding the truth of the passage. For example, you could present the main point of the passage and then show them how to mark up the text to find the support for the point. Or you could flip it and show them the support and guide them in finding the main point being supported. You could show them the structure of the passage or part of the passage and ask them how the author argues toward a conclusion.

Reports from the group is another way to cover the passage. You could have one or more learners prepare a short lesson on a specific aspect of the text. That could be background information, a word study, or a summary of any other legitimate resource you used in Chapter 6.

For some Bible passages, a **demonstration** may help make the point. When teaching the parable of the soils from Matthew 13, you could bring in different types of soil and put seeds into the soil as you walk through the verses. Teaching about judging others, you could put a log up to one eye as you read through Jesus' teaching in Matthew 7 and show how absurd it is to try to see anything when you have a log in your eye. Many word pictures from Scripture can become demonstrations in the classroom that will be especially effective for those who learn best by seeing a concrete example.

SO WHAT?

If you don't ask for input anywhere else in the lesson, I would highly recommend asking the community of learners to contribute here. As they think about the truth of the passage, ideas will occur to them that did not come up in your preparing the lesson. Use that to your benefit. That means, of course, that you will have to plan adequate time for discussing application of the truth. Here, you can have any of a variety of **discussions**. You might choose to use **brainstorming** with the entire group. You can ask them to form **buzz groups** of 3–4 learners and come up with ways the truth might be applied. You can have them discuss potential applications **one-on-one**. With any of these smaller groups, you may have them report back to the large group the best ideas they came up with.

You might also give them a **case-study** just for this part of the lesson and ask them to apply the truth to a particular situation. Being this specific in the direction of application might open up discussion to real-life situations so that they find more applications than if you ask a broad *SO WHAT?* On the other hand, it may put blinders on them so that they don't consider application outside similar situations. Knowing the capabilities of your learners can help you decide how effective this might be.

You could have them demonstrate the truth of the Word by asking some of them to **role play** for the group to see how the truth could be applied. This can lead to a discussion of effective ways to apply it. You can set up a **game** that lets them practice the truth. When the movie *O Brother, Where Art Thou?* was released, I created a game for youth called OB-stackles, named after the Blind Seer's vision of what was coming for the three main characters. The lesson was "the first shall be last and the last shall be first." In the game between two teams, they had to discover the truth and then live out helping the other team across the finish line

So What Now? — Turning it into a Lesson

— the team to have one of its players cross the line last was the winner. Years later, the youth from that group remembered the game and, hopefully, the point.

So What Now?

Remember that the point of this last part of the lesson is to have each learner commit to being transformed in some way by the truth of the passage studied. This makes the lesson very personal for them. But personal does not mean private. While no one may know the specific transformation that needs to take place in each learner, we do know that some transformation needs to take place in every learner. Being sensitive to the personal, there are many methods of achieving this.

It might be as simple as a **challenge** where you merely invite a response. It might be as extensive as connecting with an **accountability partner** to check on progress made. Or it might be something in between.

You could have them fill out a post-card with a **reminder** on it that only they would understand and then mail them the reminder a few days after the lesson to jar their memory and prick their conscience. In this age of technology, you can deliver the same type of prompt via email, text, or using any of a number of communication methods that some of us who are aging might never understand. You may ask for **progress reports** next time you meet. Rather than guilt people into moralistic behaviors, what you are trying to accomplish is motivation to be transformed and then celebration when your learners are transformed.

Done with appropriate sensitivity to how much each of us is messed up because of the fall, this part of the lesson sees transformation in the place of mere information dissemination. It is a natural follow-on to the most important question you can help them answer — *So What?*

How do you know if they are changing? In what ways can you measure the transformation the Holy Spirit is doing in them? That is the subject of the next chapter.

12

MEASURING CHANGE IN YOUR LEARNERS

Hopefully, by this point, you are preparing to teach learners not lessons. The lesson is the means of teaching the learners and the truth of the Bible is the content. How do you know if you are getting through to the learners you teach?

> The lesson is the means of teaching the learners and the truth of the Bible is the content

THE BIG PICTURE

You are engaged in the teaching portion of the Great Commission, teaching your learners to obey everything that Christ commanded. In this way, you are making disciples who know how to be disciples and, hence, live as disciples who make more disciples who know how to be disciples and live as disciples....

The big picture is that you are striving for sanctification, that is, for Christlikeness of your learners. Peter reminds us that God taught the Israelites in Leviticus 11:44, "You are to be holy, for I am holy" (1 Peter 1:16). The difficult question is, what does that look like? Fortunately, God has not left the question unanswered. Galatians 5:22–23 tells us what it looks like in a mature believer — "love, joy, peace, patience, kindness, goodness, faithfulness, gentleness, and self-control."

The fact that this fruit — not fruits — is a singular result reminds us that transformation is a holistic process. It is not like the gifts of the Spirit in which each believer has one or more ways he or she is gifted to the church. Each believer should be growing toward wholeness in all these aspects of the fruit of the Spirit.

The fact that the fruit is "of the Spirit" reminds us that the Holy Spirit is the one doing the transformation. Yet, as emphasized throughout this book, He is using you as an agent of that transformation. As a transforming teacher, you need to know if your learners are growing.

THE MEASUREMENT

As laid out in Chapter 2, we are looking for heart changes, but those are difficult-to-impossible to measure. What we can observe is head and hand changes — knowledge and behavior. And what can be observed can usually be measured. So, what do you look for in what they know and do that helps you assess their spiritual growth?

What They Know

If the big picture is obedience, your learners must know everything Christ commanded. But, Scripture is filled with more than commands. It is filled with details of the context of those commandments. Since all of Scripture is profitable, your learners need to know all of Scripture. Does that mean they need merely to memorize the content of all 66 books of the Bible? Even assuming they can do that, it is not enough. Memorization is helpful but also necessary is knowing how all that information fits together.

To help us put everything together, we have a number of tools and approaches. As introduced in Chapter 4, statements of faith help us organize the truths of Scripture into manageable chunks. Catechisms can help us learn and teach through the pairing of pertinent questions and biblical answers. More in-depth than either of these, we have systematic and biblical theology books in which experts share their views of important big-picture concepts.

BIBLICAL THEOLOGY

Biblical theology is an approach to understanding the whole of Scripture by examining the parts of redemptive history — creation, fall, redemption, and consummation — and God's progressive revelation through that history.

For example, Adam and Eve knew in Genesis 1 and 2 of God's love, but they didn't understand how far God would go to cover their sin until He killed one of the animals in Genesis 3 to clothe them while promising that a Savior would come to destroy the serpent who led them astray.

God revealed to the Israelites more details about the Savior but, until the incarnation, they did not really know who He would be.

Even at Jesus' post-resurrection ascension back into heaven, His closest disciples did not know how Jesus' work would be carried out through the church until the Holy Spirit came at Pentecost and showed them. Even then, the church didn't know the end of the story until Jesus appeared to His "beloved disciple," John, who wrote what he saw in the final book of our Bible — Revelation (not Revelations).

At each stage in redemptive history, God has revealed more about Himself. Can your learners examine a passage in its context within progressive revelation or do they, for example, still hold to the dietary laws of the Israelites because those commands are in Scripture? In other words, can they find the truth of the passage without putting themselves back under the law? Learning to live in God's grace, avoiding the extremes of legalism and licentiousness, is a sign of maturity.

> Learning to live in God's grace, avoiding the extremes of legalism and licentiousness, is a sign of maturity

SYSTEMATIC THEOLOGY

In contrast to the progressive nature of biblical theology, systematic theology examines the doctrines of the faith in their completed form. Understanding God as one and then understanding each of the three who are fully God is the beginning of systematic theology. Only with the full revelation of the entire Bible can we understand what we should know today. Understanding humanity as those who bear God's image and likeness is a doctrine explored in systematic theology. Sin and salvation (made necessary by sin) are two more doctrines or sets of doctrines covered in a typical systematic theology. Creation, heavenly and earthly, the church, and last things are still more doctrines covered in systematics. What we believe is described in the doctrines of the faith and a maturing believer will know more and more about what we believe.

What They Do

But knowing must be accompanied by doing, our faith must be put into practice as James makes clear in James 2:20 where he says that "faith without works is useless."

So What Now? — Turning it into a Lesson

How do we know that our learners want to grow? The simple answer is that they are doing something about it. Practicing the spiritual disciplines is a way that we make ourselves available to the Holy Spirit so that He can sanctify us. Reading, studying, meditating on, and then applying the Bible is the way we individually hear from God. Hearing the Word preached and taught is the primary way we take in the Bible as a church. Praying is the way we speak to God, who has loved us enough to reveal Himself to us. Worship, evangelism, serving the body of Christ and those outside the body, stewardship of the resources — time, talents, and treasure — God has entrusted to us, fasting, periods of silence, and journaling are all ways that we can become more disciplined disciples. Do you see evidence of a growing desire to grow in your learners? If so, do you see evidence that they are growing?

Jesus said the greatest two commandments are "love God" and "love those who bear God's image." These two summarize the Beatitudes (Matthew 5:2–12) at the beginning of Jesus' Sermon on the Mount (Matthew 5–7), which, itself, is a detailed description of righteous living. Of course, Jesus is the only one who ever lived out God's righteousness perfectly and only by having His righteousness credited to us can we be reconciled to God. But God does more than credit Jesus' righteousness to those who believe on Him and trust His work to save them; God actually conforms us to that righteousness so that we do love God and love others. Those loves, those affections, are demonstrated. Two good measures of this kind of growth are priorities and prayer requests.

Growing disciples have a change in priority from self to others. What do you hear them talk about as they enter class? What illustrations do they resonate with in the lesson? How do they apply the truths of God's word? If they are consistently self-centered, they are likely immature in their faith. If they are consistently other-centered, you have a good clue their hearts are changing.

> Growing disciples have a change in priority from self to others

There is probably no better place to see the contrast of self-centered and other-centered than in their prayer requests. Immature believers tend to focus on the organ recital (my heart, my mom's lungs, my uncle's kidneys, etc.), the financial audit (I'm not sure whether I should buy this house, this car, etc.), and the travel

> There is probably no better place to see the contrast of self-centered and other-centered than in their prayer requests

itinerary (traveling mercies for my upcoming trip). In short, they focus on the effects of sin. While these are important and should be prayed for, maturing disciples pray for more. They grieve for sin — personal and global. They are broken when they sin; they grieve that loved ones remain lost; they envision the salvation of people far and near that they have not yet met. In other words, they are other-centered more than self-centered. They long to see every person as God sees them and then strive to do something to help them be conformed to Christ, to make disciples.

What your learners know and what they do are measures of their transformation. Are you in a close enough relationship with them that you can recognize these changes when they occur? If not, how could you change? How can you be more other-centered? How can you improve your effectiveness as a called and equipped teacher in the church? That is the subject of the next chapter.

13

PLANNING FOR CHANGE IN YOUR TEACHING

Just as you plan to see transformation in your learners, you as the teacher are being transformed. Part of your transformation is improving your teaching.

They say, "practice makes perfect." Whoever this mysterious *They* is and no matter how often what *They* know isn't actually true, they are almost correct on this one. Your teaching is unlikely to improve if you don't actually practice. Even if you could know everything about the biblical text and everything about your learners and even everything about teaching methods, you will not know how effective your teaching is until you teach and see learners learn, until you see them transformed by the work the Holy Spirit has called and equipped you to do.

One way to improve your teaching is to pay attention to your learners. During the lesson, does it seem like they understand what you want them to understand? Are they motivated to allow themselves to be transformed by the truth of the teaching point? After the lesson, do they give evidence of transformation? If not, you need to determine where you may have failed in teaching your learners. Perhaps you have fallen into the temptation to teach the lesson rather than the learners. Maybe you have delivered facts — or even truth — without calling them to be transformed by it. You may be teaching at a level or with a method that is ineffective for them. Whatever the reason, you need to know so that you can improve rather than blame them for your failure.

> One way to improve your teaching is to pay attention to your learners

Probably the most effective way of knowing if your teaching is transformational is to submit yourself to critical evaluation. I know that just the suggestion to be critiqued can make you cringe. Get over it! If you are called to teach, you should want to teach well and, no matter how long you have taught, you need to improve.

> Probably the most effective way of knowing if your teaching is transformational is to submit yourself to critical evaluation

So What Now? — Turning it into a Lesson

I have found that nothing makes you more diligent in your preparation and lesson delivery than knowing that someone is critically watching you. I have included an evaluation form at the back of this book that has been useful for me and for those I teach to teach. The form can be completed by your learners, by other teachers or other church leaders who sit in on your lesson for the primary purpose of evaluating your teaching or, better, by a combination of these. The evaluation form overrides the inclination to give you a reflexive *attaboy* rather than reflective help.

Take a look and you will see that the evaluation centers on the Effective Four — *Why? • What? • So What? • So What Now?* That is not out of laziness or a lack of imagination on my part. Instead, it is based on my conviction that these are the important questions to help your learners answer and, if you are teaching to those answers, they should be able to answer them.

As you review the feedback you receive from them, don't congratulate yourself on their positive comments or castigate yourself on their negative feedback. Instead, hear what they claim to have derived from the lesson and compare that to your teaching plan. Do their answers indicate that you accomplished your aims? Did they understand the teaching point you gleaned from all your work in the Word? Did they feel compelled to be transformed by that truth? At what point(s) in the lesson did they seem most engaged? How does that compare to what you know about your learners or inform you about what you need to know about them? Based on what you now know about them, how can you teach more effectively?

> Don't congratulate yourself on positive comments or castigate yourself on negative feedback

If you risk being assessed by others, don't make it a one-off effort. Instead, build into your heart the need and the value of coming under scrutiny. Then, change your practice so that you regularly seek feedback. If we build our teaching cadre to expect critique, you can offer to serve other teachers in this way.

Since the fall in Genesis 3 affects everything we are and everything we do, I need to issue one more caution. Don't play to the audience of enrolled critics. That is, don't save your best methods and cleverest quips for the times you are being evaluated. Strive to improve so the Audience of One — the Lord whose bride you teach — is pleased. He is worthy of your best efforts. We are being used so that the bride is made beautiful, preparing to be presented to her bridegroom spotless.

> Strive to improve so the Audience of One — the Lord whose bride you teach — is pleased

It is love for that bride and Bridegroom that this book was written.

Teach well.

Additional Resources for

Turning it into a Lesson

For More Study of Teaching Methods

- Hendricks, Howard. *Teaching to Change Lives: Seven Proven Ways to Make Your Teaching Come Alive*. Colorado Springs: Multnomah Books, 1987.
- Richards, Lawrence O., and Gary J. Bredfeldt. *Creative Bible Teaching,* Rev. & Upd. Chicago, IL: Moody Publishers, 2020.
- Zuck, Roy B. *Teaching as Jesus Taught*. Grand Rapids, MI: Baker Book House, 1995.
- Zuck, Roy B. *Teaching as Paul Taught*. Grand Rapids, MI: Baker Book House, 1998.

For More Study of Measures of Change

- Barna, George. *Growing True Disciples: New Strategies for Producing Genuine Followers of Christ*. Colorado Springs, CO: WaterBrook Press, 2001.
- Geiger, Eric, Michael Kelley, and Philip Nation. *Transformational Discipleship: How People Really Grow*. Nashville, TN: B&H Publishing Group, 2012.
- Ogden, Greg. *Transforming Discipleship: Making Disciples a Few at a Time*, Rev. & Exp. Downers Grove, IL: IVP Books, 2016.

For More Study of Knowledge-Related Topics

- Erickson, Millard J., *Christian Theology,* 3rd ed. Grand Rapids, MI: Baker Academic, 2013.
- Grudem, Wayne. *Systematic Theology: An Introduction to Biblical Doctrine*, 2nd ed.. Grand Rapids, MI: Zondervan, 2020.
- Hamilton, James M. Jr. *God's Glory in Salvation through Judgment: A Biblical Theology.* Wheaton, IL: Crossway, 2010.
- Hamilton, James M. Jr. *What is Biblical Theology?: A Guide to the Bible's Story, Symbolism, and Patterns.* Wheaton, IL: Crossway, 2013.
- Lawrence, Michael. *Biblical Theology in the Life of the Church: A Guide for Ministry.* Wheaton, IL: Crossway, 2010.
- MacArthur, John, and Richard Mayhue. *Biblical Doctrine: A Systematic Summary of Bible Truth.* Wheaton, IL: Crossway, 2017.

For More Study of Practice-Related Topics

- Hawkins, Greg L. and & Cally Parkinson. *Follow Me: What's Next for You?* Barrington, IL: Willow Creek Association, 2008.
- Whitney, Donald S. *Spiritual Disciplines for the Christian Life*, Rev. & Upd. Colorado Springs, CO, 2014.

EXPANDING TO BIGGER PROJECTS

The Effective Four is good beyond a single Bible lesson. Following the pattern — *WHY? • WHAT? • SO WHAT? • SO WHAT NOW?* — helps you organize several lessons that could make up a single course or several courses that combine to be a curriculum of study. And this doesn't just apply to single Bible passages. In this section, I am going to show you how to apply the principles to a topical study, how to go from solid content that you may have gathered from deep study of some topic to a course that is organized in a way to make your learners wise rather than merely better informed.

Then, I am going to show you how to apply the Effective Four to a curriculum that combines several courses into an organized plan that keeps wisdom as the goal.

14

PLANNING A MULTI-LESSON COURSE

Sometimes, you're not teaching a specific Bible passage. Instead, you may have been asked to teach on a topic that would be helpful for the church. That could be a lesson on a doctrine of the church, an overview of one of the Testaments, some part of church history, something practical like family discipleship, or some other topic that takes you outside a single passage of Scripture. Let's assume you've taken notes and come up with some solid content you want to teach. How do you turn that knowledge-based content into a lesson that teaches wisdom?

If you consider the order of preparing a lesson taught in this book, you have already taken care of the *WHAT?* ... maybe.

WHY?

The first question you need to ask is, "What heart change would I hope to see in my learners as a result of the lesson or lessons?" If you're just aiming at filling their heads with knowledge, you need to take another look at the previous chapters to see why that's a bad idea. How would you want their hearts changed? What change would you want to see in their loves, their affections, their attitudes... and then their volition, the choices that come out of those affections.

Jesus taught in the Sermon on the Mount that where your treasure is, there your heart will be also. Consider how you can organize your lesson or lessons to help them treasure the things of God so that their hearts will be made more Christlike. What commitment could you expect they will make as a result of your teaching? Once you've determined the commitment you want them to make toward Christlikeness, then you're ready to determine the content they need to move them to make that commitment.

What?

That's where you may need to adjust your content. Do you have 2 hours of content and 45 minutes to teach it? Well, don't try to fit it in. You may think that you're helping them by giving them more content than they need, but that's like the old "drinking from a firehose" picture. Drowning them in information is not teaching.

Instead, give them a drink of the truth. So, consider what single point you think is central to the change you want to see in them. Then, teach that single point well. Instead of the standard "Three points and an illustration," which can feel like the firehose, consider making one point and supporting it with whatever content they need to change their hearts. You may need to come up with an activity they could do that would drive the lesson home. That may be an activity that helps them discover your main point of the lesson or it may be an activity that helps them see the value and application of that main point.

So What?

Whatever you're teaching and however you're teaching it, keep wisdom in mind. How do you see them becoming wiser as a result of the lesson? That should be your goal in teaching anyone anything. If they are not better equipped to live in reality, you are wasting both your time and theirs by teaching new knowledge or new skills.

You can formalize the lesson plan by listing your learning aims. Your affective aim is the heart change you want to see in them. Your cognitive aim is the main point of the lesson that could result in that heart change. Your behavioral aim is the activity you might use to drive home the main point or it could be what they do after committing to being changed by the lesson. Even if you don't formalize the lesson plan, you need to keep these aims in mind as you prepare and as you teach.

So What Now?

Then, consider how you could call for a commitment to the change you anticipate. If they do something as seemingly insignificant as silently answering the question, "Would you commit to this right now?", they have made a commitment toward being wise. They are more likely to follow through. You can increase that possibility by having them do something physical — raise their hand, move to a place along a wall representing their degree of commitment, write down their commitment, etc. You can increase their level of commitment even more by building in some sort of accountability — report back next time, accountability partner, etc.

METHOD

In preparing to teach, you need to consider how to use your time with them. Is lecture the best method? What if you built in discussion around the application? Or, what if you included a case study? Or a role play? You might provide them a worksheet and then help them discover the content rather than just have them fill in blanks on a page. There are many ways to teach and the way they learn best may not be the way you prefer to teach. Consider who you are doing the lesson for. If it is for your good and your glory, teach the way you prefer. If it is for their good and God's glory, consider how they prefer to learn.

15

PLANNING A MULTI-COURSE CURRICULUM

Often, a single lesson from an extended passage or a single lesson on a topic is not sufficient. How do you construct a series of lessons so that the entire course is aimed at making your learners wise? Here are some things to consider.

WHY?

First, why are you teaching the course? How do you hope their hearts will be changed as a result of learning everything in the series?

WHAT?

Once you know how you anticipate the Holy Spirit changing them, you can settle on how you are going to divide the content. For example, if you are teaching an introduction to the Old Testament, would you divide by the canonical divisions: history, writings, and prophets? Would you divide the content in canonical order: starting with Genesis and ending with Malachi? Would you divide the content around the timing of the exile of Judah into Babylon: covering pre-exile history, writings, and prophets and then post-exile history, writings, and prophets? Your divisions should reflect the heart change you are wanting to see in them. Then, the content of each lesson could be designed to support the overall structure and heart change you are wanting to see.

SO WHAT?

Each lesson should have one main point that supports your overall purpose for the course. Within the structure, you could focus on knowledge, affections, and behaviors in different combinations within each lesson. Think about which lessons are better suited to each of these learning domains — head, heart, and hands. Knowing what you are trying to cover as a result of the teaching series gives you flexibility in designing each lesson. It also allows you flexibility in how you will teach each lesson. You might start with a content-intense lecture in the first lesson and end with a role-playing application in the final lesson. The point

15

PLANNING A MULTI-COURSE CURRICULUM

Often, a single lesson from an extended passage or a single lesson on a topic is not sufficient. How do you construct a series of lessons so that the entire course is aimed at making your learners wise? Here are some things to consider.

WHY?

First, why are you teaching the course? How do you hope their hearts will be changed as a result of learning everything in the series?

WHAT?

Once you know how you anticipate the Holy Spirit changing them, you can settle on how you are going to divide the content. For example, if you are teaching an introduction to the Old Testament, would you divide by the canonical divisions: history, writings, and prophets? Would you divide the content in canonical order: starting with Genesis and ending with Malachi? Would you divide the content around the timing of the exile of Judah into Babylon: covering pre-exile history, writings, and prophets and then post-exile history, writings, and prophets? Your divisions should reflect the heart change you are wanting to see in them. Then, the content of each lesson could be designed to support the overall structure and heart change you are wanting to see.

SO WHAT?

Each lesson should have one main point that supports your overall purpose for the course. Within the structure, you could focus on knowledge, affections, and behaviors in different combinations within each lesson. Think about which lessons are better suited to each of these learning domains — head, heart, and hands. Knowing what you are trying to cover as a result of the teaching series gives you flexibility in designing each lesson. It also allows you flexibility in how you will teach each lesson. You might start with a content-intense lecture in the first lesson and end with a role-playing application in the final lesson. The point is that by expanding beyond a single lesson, you can mix things up as you strive to reach your overall objective of teaching wisdom.

So What Now?

As with any lessons you teach, you should have a main point and learning aims for each lesson. These may be formally spelled out or they may be informal, appearing nowhere other than your mind. But you need to do the work of setting learning aims so that you know what to include ... and so that you know what you can leave out. You can't cover everything you know, so you have to decide what has priority. And, this priority needs to support the whole series, the course you are teaching. So, the whole series should have its own learning aims. At the end of the course, what heart changes do you want to see? What content could be presented that would achieve that heart change? What activities might contribute to the heart change or reflect the heart changes you want? The answer to those questions help you organize the whole so that each piece fits together.

Curriculum Instead of a Course

If you absolutely have more content than you can cover in the number of lessons allotted, consider dividing the course into two separate courses that, of course, would fit together in a coordinated way. This bottom-up approach could be extended to an overall curriculum for a group of learners. Alternatively, you could start at the top, make choices about the kinds of things to teach, and then work your way down to the individual courses that could be included to support your overall curriculum. Either way, you could then decide a level at which to teach various courses.

For example, you might have some introductory courses that, combined, constitute what you would consider a core curriculum for your church — the major ideas they should know about to grow as disciples of Christ. From this core, you could have more specific courses that drill down into more and more advanced courses. Educators call this a scope-and-sequence. The scope is the range of topics; the sequence is the order of teaching within each topic that builds toward ever-increasing wisdom.

So, you might have a core curriculum of 7 big topics that you want to introduce. Then, within each of those 7, you could add more advanced courses that help your learners grow even deeper in the Word. If you find that there are courses you would want to teach but they don't fit neatly within your big 7, you might reconsider your choice of the 7 main topics.

All of this design follows the Effective Four: *WHY?* • *WHAT?* • *SO WHAT?* • *SO WHAT NOW?*

WHY? do you want them to know? *WHAT?* do they need to know to get there? *SO WHAT?* can you provide that will set them up for success in learning everything they need? And *SO WHAT NOW?* What courses, objectives, and main points do you need to include that makes the best use of your time together?

REAL-LIFE EXAMPLE

Let's walk through a real-life example. This comes from a team I worked with at a church several years ago. Our team decided that the 7 core ideas that we needed were related to: the Bible, the church, doctrine, discipleship, spiritual disciplines, family, and mission.

Once we had those divisions made, we came up with a rough draft of a description of each course. We didn't settle on the final version of the course description until the design process was near its end.

With a draft of the course descriptions, we determined what the overall objectives were for each course, starting with the affective aims, the heart changes we thought were likely in each course.

Then, we decided on cognitive aims, the knowledge they would need to achieve the heart changes.

Finally, we decided on the behavioral aims, what might be done in the lessons to achieve the heart changes as well as the behaviors we anticipated that would demonstrate the heart changes had occurred.

EXPANDING TO BIGGER PROJECTS

We located resources that we thought would be helpful in preparing and teaching the lessons and we divided the proposed content into 6 lessons for each of the 7 core courses. Each lesson had its own big idea that supported the aims of the course.

Along the way, we tried to settle on a key Bible passage that we thought captured the essence of what we were trying to accomplish in each course.

Here is what we came up with in our 6-week course on the church.

Our course description was finalized as: "To bring glory to God, we must relate to His people as God intended. Throughout the ages there has been confusion about the definition and function of the church. This course will help the student understand how the universal church is expressed in the local congregation so that membership fulfills God's purpose for the body."

The description of each course followed this pattern: How we understand we are supposed to bring glory to God. What we saw as the biggest specific problem in doing that. Then, what the course was designed to contribute to the solution to that problem.

Our key passage for the course on the church was Acts 2:42–47, which reads, "They devoted themselves to the apostles' teaching, to the fellowship, to the breaking of bread, and to prayer. Everyone was filled with awe, and many wonders and signs were being performed through the apostles. Now all the believers were together and held all things in common. They sold their possessions and property and distributed the proceeds to all, as any had need. Every day they devoted themselves to meeting together in the temple, and broke bread from house to house. They ate their food with joyful and sincere hearts, praising God and enjoying the favor of all the people. Every day the Lord added to their number those who were being saved."

Our affective learning aim was:
▶ The learner will appreciate the benefit and responsibility of being a member of the body of Christ.

To support that heart change, our three cognitive aims were:
- ▶ The learner will understand the way the local church relates to the larger body of Christ throughout the world and across time.
- ▶ The learner will know the necessity and benefits of membership in the body of Christ.
- ▶ The learner will understand the two ordinances of the church.

Then, the behavioral aims we thought would demonstrate their appreciation of the benefits and responsibilities were:
- ▶ The learner will participate in the benefits of membership.
- ▶ The learner will actively pursue a work of ministry

The 6-lesson outline came from the big ideas we thought would achieve our affective aim:
  I. God's kingdom is demonstrated by the church
  II. God's Word is obeyed by the church
  III. God's unity is reflected by the church
  IV. God's provision is celebrated by the church
  V. God's praise is proclaimed by the church
  VI. God's commission is carried out by the church

And the resources we found helpful in design and thought would be helpful in teaching the course were:
- ▶ Dever, Mark. *What is a Healthy Church?* Wheaton, IL: Crossway, 2007.
- ▶ Grudem, Wayne A. "Part VI: The Doctrine of the Church." In *Bible Doctrine: Essentials Teachings of the Christian Faith*. Edited by Jeff Purswell. Grand Rapids, MI: Zondervan, 1999.
- ▶ Leeman, Jonathan. *Church Membership: How the World Knows Who Represents Jesus*. Building Healthy Churches. Wheaton, IL: Crossway, 2012

Your choices in each of these matters may differ from ours, but the process should still be applied. Remember that your goal is to teach wisdom. You cannot teach it all in a lifetime, much less a single lesson. But, each time you gather, you could move each of your learners a bit closer to wisdom in how they love God and love God's image-bearers.

Resources & Helps

Worksheets on the following pages can be helpful as you complete your Bible study and prepare to teach your learners. The latest version of the worksheets can be found at TeachersOfTheBible.org.

OBSERVATION WORKSHEET

Passage: Primary Translation:
                                Other Translations:

What words, phrases, sentences, or explanations seem unclear?

Are there additional questions that arise from comparing translations?

What are the repeated words/phrases?

What connecting words (e.g., but, to, therefore) does the author use?

Do there seem to be comparisons or contrasts?

Is there an apparent timeline or geographical progression?

Is there a truth with an application for the original readers?

What type of writing (genre) is the passage (e.g., narrative, drama, discourse, parable, proverb, poem, prophecy, apocalypse)?

Resources & Helps

STRUCTURE WORKSHEET

Passage:

[copy the entire passage; leave the words in order, but align the text so that the author's main idea(s) is(are) on the left side of the page and supporting ideas under the word/phrase they support]

Context Worksheet

Passage:

How does the passage fit into the sentences and paragraphs immediately around the passage?

How does the passage fit into the book as a whole?

How does the passage fit within the Testament in which it occurs?

INTERPRETATION WORKSHEET

Passage: Genre:

What is the big idea of this passage (e.g., what did it mean to the original readers/hearers)?

Is this big idea explained elsewhere in Scripture? If so, what other passages either explain better or support your interpretation of this passage?

Moving outside the time of the original readers, what is the truth communicated in the big idea of this passage that is true across all time and in every place and culture?

Lesson Plan Template

Passage:
Special Needs of Learners:

Aims:
  Affective:

  Cognitive:

  Behavioral:

Classroom Setup:

Why?:

Transition:

What?:

So What?:

So What Now?:

TEACHING FEEDBACK FORM

What do you need to know? What was the main point?

How did the teacher support that point?

Why do you need to know this?

How engaged were you as a learner? Why do you think that was?

How convinced were you that the main point being made was actually true?

What change were you encouraged to consider? How does the main point apply to you today?

What specific thing were you called to do?

What did the teacher do well in teaching?

What might the teacher do to improve?

Course Development

Title of Course

Key Verse(s):

Course Description: [How does this topic bring glory to God?] [What has gone wrong that interferes with us glorifying God in this?] [How will this course provide a solution to that problem?]

Objectives/Aims:
    Affective Aim:

    Cognitive Aim(s):

    Behavioral Aim(s):

Outline:
    I. Lesson 1 topic
        A. Learning objectives/aims (affective, cognitive, and/or behavioral)

        B. *WHY?*: Draw the learners into the lesson

        C. *WHAT?*: Main point
            1. Support for the main point
            2. Additional support for the main point

        D. *So WHAT?*: How might this lesson be applied?
           How does this lesson fit into the whole course?

        E. *So WHAT NOW?*: What specific commitment could they make that would achieve the aim(s) for this lesson and achieve the overall aims for the course?
    II. Lesson 2, etc.

Useful Resources:
- Resource 1
- Resource 2

Made in the USA
Middletown, DE
24 April 2022